Natural Born
The Life of
Jack Johnson

by Marc Shapiro

First edition published in 2006 by
Helter Skelter Publishing
South Bank House
Black Prince Road
London SE1 7SJ

www.helterskelterpublishing.com

Copyright 2006 © Marc Shapiro
All rights reserved

Typesetting and layout by Graeme Milton
Cover design by Chris Wilson
Printed in Great Britain by CPI, Bath

All lyrics quoted in this book are for the purposes of review, study or criticism.

The right of the author to be identified as author of this work has been asserted in accordance with the Copyright, Design and Patents Act, 1988.

All rights reserved. No part of this publication may be transmitted in any form, or by any means, electronic, photocopying, recording, or otherwise, without the prior permission of the publisher.

This book is sold subject to the condition that it shall not, by way of trade or otherwise, be lent, resold, hired out or otherwise circulated without the publisher's prior consent in any form of binding or cover other than that in which it is published and without a similar condition including this condition being imposed on the subsequent purchase.

A CIP record for this book is available from the British Library

ISBN-10 1-905139-14-4
ISBN-13 978-1-9051-3914-9

Natural Born Man:
The Life of
Jack Johnson

by Marc Shapiro

Helter Skelter publishing

Contents

Introduction

The Jack Johnson Equation

Jack Johnson is a musical anomaly of the first order.

Stylistically, and in his approach to singing and songwriting, the Hawaiian-born Johnson is light years removed from the carbon copy alternative rock, the often overbearing and ultimately shallow hip-hop/rap scene and the pre-fab pretty face pop acts that dominate the popular music scene.

Johnson enjoys the idea that his music is so far out of the accepted mainstream and is often the butt of his own jokes centered around his non-conformist style. He has likened himself to the pickled ginger to everyone else's sushi, something between different tastes to mellow the palette out. He has also acknowledged quite candidly that his mellow music is the logical break from all the angry and aggressive rock that dots the landscape.

And because his music is so totally leftfield in conception and presentation, it is often hard to find. Even this late in the game, there are still some top forty stations that won't play him. Unless it's a station with progressive roots or a small wattage college station or one with an easy listening bent, a good portion of the stations on the FM dial will find Jack Johnson's music missing in action.

Name recognition? It's largely more of the same. Mention that he's the surfer who sings and you might get a nod or two of recognition. But mention him simply by name in the non hip, pop culture savvy world, and you might get the proverbial 'Jack who?' or an aside to the black boxer Jack Johnson or, for the more esoteric, the blues legend Big Jack Johnson.

So to a large degree, nobody knows him. But in a sly, seductive way, he's one of the world's reigning pop commodities.

Jack Johnson's arrival on the music scene might not be an act of God but it is definitely a breath of fresh air during what has become quite cynical times in the pop music world. Music in the 90s and well into 2006 has become a loss leader; a way to move into an acting career, book deals and clothing lines. And it shows in cookie cutter sounds geared towards radio playlists, demographics and all those soulless, big money elements that put the business in music business.

That is not Jack Johnson's way. Refreshingly and legitimately naïve to the business side of things. The closest thing there is to a Jack Johnson clothing line is the ecologically friendly and reasonably priced T-shirts and caps he sells at his concerts. He is so private that a book deal, at least to this point, is out of the question. When it comes to his reason for being, his music, he is not running it through a committee or a bank of Pro Tools technology.

With Jack Johnson it's an all or nothing proposition. Love the music or hate it. It all begins and ends with the music. And it is all quite contrary to the business ethic. If his music is top forty fodder, it is purely by accident. Outside of a handful of videos and a goof guest shot in the movie Out Cold, Johnson has no designs on acting. If there's a book in him, it has not happened yet. A clothing line? You've got to be kidding. But at the end of the day, Jack Johnson, unlike almost all of his pop music contemporaries, wins out by virtue of being real.

Explanations aside, what makes Jack Johnson so intrinsically alien is the pure simplicity of what he does. And it is that simplicity that makes him a breath of fresh air.

The equation is an easy one. One man. One guitar. Heartfelt, meditative and often quite personal lyrics about life, love and loss. A soft folk-soul-blues sung in a passionate, yet subtle, white man's voice. All of which is finally wrapped up in a sandals-and-cut-offs island vibe that literally oozes bohemian-hippie attitudes of escape and idyllic natural existence.

This is like Haight Ashbury if Altamont, hard drugs and even harder vibes had never happened. It's 60s-style psychedelia morphed into a much simpler place. Listening to Jack Johnson ply his trade, one can almost smell the essence of bud in the air, the easy laughs and conversations around a beach side bonfire and a timeless place far removed from reality.

In a nutshell, that's Jack.

Jack Johnson is a much deeper specimen than most critics have given him credit for being. He is not the 'Surf-Folkie', the easy caricature given his roots and laidback ways. There is nothing remotely Beach Boys or Dick Dale about him. He is not the poor man's Don Ho (although one of his most popular songs, 'Bubble Toes' does play in the same emotional shallows as Ho's 'Tiny Bubbles') nor is he Jimmy Buffet's island cousin (despite having recently covered the Buffet song 'A Pirate Looks At Forty'). Jack Johnson's roots go much deeper than that.

Johnson's influences lay deep in the soil of late 30s and early 40s Americana when country and blues merged into what would become a a flourishing era of modern folk when performers like Jimmy Rodgers and Woody Guthrie gave new meaning to the term 'A man and his guitar.' In fact, Johnson often points to the discovery of a battered Woody Guthrie album bought in a low rent Hawaiian thrift shop as a defining moment in his musical education.

There is also much of the 60s folk movement present in Johnson's music; especially in those moments when the singer-songwriter chooses to take on environmental and social issues in songs like 'Good People' and 'The Horizon Has Been Defeated'. His quiet, forceful tones resonate with the ghosts of a non-nasal Dylan and a somewhat less country Arlo Guthrie. There is no escaping the fact that, in his moments of playful, goodtime, there is more than a nod to The Grateful Dead and all their offshoots and permutations in the jam band world. Johnson is not without his jazz roots and at any given time one hears a suggestion of Mose Allison in the air. His 'heavy friends' have also had an influence on Johnson as his sly, sexual smoothness is nothing if not a nod and a wink to G. Love And Special Sauce and Ben Harper.

Johnson, quite naturally, has worshipped at the musical shrine of all the greats and, with an acknowledgement to the past, has made his music distinctively his own.

So that, long and short, is the ramp up to *Natural Born Man: The Life Of Jack Johnson*, an odyssey into what goes into making a quiet, soft spoken rebel in an often not so rebellious world. If you've gotten this far, chances are you're already a fan. Or maybe you just bought into the hype and are Curious Johnson. You've bought his CDs and experienced Jack Johnson live in a concert setting that offers up the ambiance of a living room show for a few beer-soaked friends. Or you've caught the cat on the radio a time or two but haven't sprung for the whole load. You are the choir this book is preaching to or you're a stranger in this strange land. You know the cat has talent, a timeless talent if you will. Or you know squat and just want to know more. For either side of the Jack Johnson fence there is more to the world of Jack Johnson than mere talent. So much more.

Jack Johnson is a pop star without all the expected pop star baggage. Serial adultery, alcoholic fits, nights of debauchery and the sticking of that old devil junk in his veins? Jack Johnson has done none of those things. Believe me, I looked. If it was there, I would have found it.

There is no question that anybody young and single, given the choice between going on the road with Kiss or Jack Johnson, would go with Kiss everytime. And that would not bother Johnson in the least. For his music and his lifestyle is a bit more mature and, darest we say it, a bit more settled than the typical rock and roll circus.

To a large extent, Jack Johnson fans have sewn their wild oats. They're old hippies with laidback souls who like a night out to remember the time. And in a nice, mellow, laidback setting, that is what Jack Johnson provides them.

Or, at the other end of the spectrum, they are young and idealistic people who are seeking peace and serenity in the sand, surf and isolated outposts of the world. And finally, they are the urban dwellers, those trapped in a lifestyle not necessarily of their own making who are, quite simply, looking for escape. In Jack Johnson all these factions have found a fellow traveller.

The worst thing you can say about Jack Johnson is that he rises at an early, non-rock star hour and makes his wife an avocado and egg sandwich for breakfast. If you're really looking for dirt, I have it on good authority that he will occasionally perform in a T-shirt that has not been washed in eight days. So, if you're looking for sleaze and all manner of tell-all, you've come to the wrong place. However, being the kind of person you could bring home to mom and dad does not translate into boring. Far from it.

For the excitement in the life and times of Jack Johnson truly rests in his art and the passion in which he pursues it. A true renaissance man, Johnson has, over the years, moved quietly and with determination in and out of his passions. From surfing to documentary filmmaking to music and, as the wind takes him, back again; Johnson has taken his life's joys in true bohemian fashion. Never offering up a nose-to-the-grindstone attitude but, ultimately, showing off a natural, easygoing devotion to each. Johnson does not so much have a career as he does an ever expanding series of hobbies; creative moments that he indulges at his own whim and at his own speed.

And make no mistake, that speed can be maddeningly slow and predictable in a world that is anything but. He records, he tours, he surfs, he hangs out with wife, child, family and friends. Those who have chosen to document Jack Johnson journalistically can vouch for the fact that, except for talking about a new album or tour, Johnson's responses to questions and the attempts to get behind the performer to the man are pretty much of a continuous loop; retracing old steps and revealing little.

And this is not some cloak and dagger operation on the part of Johnson. It is just the performer reveling in and revealing a world that may seem limiting but is nothing if not comfortable.

Jack Johnson could not make it in the world most of us live in. He could not have a boss because he would never think of working for somebody else unless there was an easy escape clause. You could not get him to dress the part most of us do on a daily basis. He's not someone who lives and dies by his answer machine. Point of fact: he has one but he rarely listens to messages and almost never returns calls. In our world, Jack Johnson would be fired on the spot. His is the only world that will have him.

Don't look for the odd quirk or unexpected blow-up. He is so even keel about his life and career to the point of madness for those who, for better or worse, live a complex, high-speed existence. Which ultimately may be what makes Jack Johnson such an enjoyable experience. It's kind of fun to be around somebody who you know will never develop an ulcer or lay awake nights for the wrong reason.

Jack Johnson is one happy cat. And an eternally grateful one at that. Rarely an interview goes by without the singer professing how happy he is for everything that's happened to him. And yeah, everybody thanks everybody including God at the often interminable awards shows. But with

Jack Johnson the thanks for the good fortune is quite sincere. The man actually comes close to apologising for his good luck which, occasionally, does come close to pressing the pretentious button. My feeling is you've earned it, enjoy it. Just don't tell me you're sorry.

Besides, the guilt for his good fortune is more than balanced out by his endless good works. This is a performer who gives back at every opportunity. If there's a cause, where does he sign up. If it's for the planet, he's there in spades. If some schoolkids at a local elementary school need some schooling on the realities of recycling, Johnson will be there. He is not the type for a soup kitchen photo op or the calculated writing of a cheque. Is he sincere about his good works? Most definitely.

And because he has been able to so intricately combine his art with the realities of commerce, he has been in the enviable position of being able to stick it to the man when the mood strikes him. Johnson tends to fly above it all when it comes to his business dealings with the corporate arm of the music biz. Over the years, he has routinely blown off important meetings with producers and label executives and his excuses are outrageous in their cander.

Quite simply Jack Johnson is a man of the water and the simple moments with wife, child, friends and surf are more important than the dollars and cents of recording sessions and the logistics of touring. Make no mistake, in his own way the business is important to him and it always gets taken care of in its own time. But give Jack Johnson the choice of catching a wave at some far flung part of the world or sifting through the minutiae and fine print of a contract... Well it really is no contest.

Jack Johnson is, indeed, a natural born man. It's in his music. Sincerity. Honesty. Simplicity in a surf against the shore timeless manner that most flavours of the month will never know or understand.

If you examine anything in enough detail, it will come out appearing complex. And if all of the above makes Jack Johnson appear to be even remotely complex, I apologise. Because Jack Johnson at his core is fairly predictable, fairly simple in his outlook and, to the world outside his bubble that moves at a much faster pace than he does, he might appear not all that interesting. The life of Jack Johnson moves in cycles that often repeat themselves. Which is why a biography of Jack Johnson will never approach the thickness of *War and Peace*. He's not the Beatles, he's not the Rolling Stones. He has not had that kind of life. But to be sure, he has had a life worth examining.

I don't know what Jack Johnson's reaction will be to this book. Given what my research shows, he most likely will resent the intrusion. He might also be sheepishly embarrassed that somebody would go to all the trouble to write a book about a life he considered so ordinary and insignificant. More likely, he might just shrug the notion off with a laugh and a roll of his eyes.

Natural Born Man: The Life Of Jack Johnson is a true reflection on a man of simple passions and tastes who has managed to marry his feelings about all the big and small moments in life to an infectious acoustic beat. Jack Johnson is finally a man true to his visions and generous enough to invite us along for the ride.

Jack Johnson would rather be surfing. And at the end of the day, so would we all.

Marc Shapiro 2006

01

Business 101: Just Say No

This is how Jack Johnson does business.

One day Johnson was sitting in the plush office of a big time record company executive. You know the type; outwardly hip, with just the right amount of bling and a firm grasp on the lingo of the day, with a not too veiled veneer of corporate on the cusp. It was the late 90s and word was already beginning to leak out about the Hawaiian-born kid with the oh so mellow sound. In tape trading circles that easily rivalled and perhaps surpassed the exploits of Deadheads, Jack Johnson was already being hailed as 'The King Of Surf-Folk'. The more manic in their devotion to this newfound sage of surf and song in their devotion were calling him the new Woody Guthrie, the new Bob Dylan and the new Beach Boys all in the same breath.

If hype could kill, Jack Johnson was already dead.

Jack Johnson was not exactly what the music industry was looking for. Paper thin teen idols who could not sing, cookie cutter *American Idol* divas with the ability to sing bland, forgettable ballads and angst-ridden alternative rockers processed through Pro Tools technology were the genres that were selling and with their herd mentality, labels were looking for more of the same. Jack Johnson could not be those things if he tried. But major labels were being drawn to the hyperbole like sharks to a blood slick.

Chris Mauro, a long time confidant of Johnson's and editor of *Surfer*

Magazine, had heard the stories of that meeting and they went something like this:

'This guy wanted to sign him right away,' recalled Mauro in a 2005 interview. 'He said, "If you sign this, you'll be touring 200 nights a year." Jack said, "Well how about 100 nights a year?" And the guy says, "How soon can you get into the studio?" Jack said, "I don't know. I'm going on a surf trip next month." Now the guy is starting to get real upset and he said, "Wait! I'm sitting here telling you that I want to make you a star and you're giving me these excuses?" Well the truth was that Jack really did not care.'

And no, this was not some business ploy designed to drive up the offer and to meet some outrageous asking price.

On the contrary, Jack Johnson cared very much. Too much to even think of tying himself down to a major label deal. Because when it came to creative harmony and the cold, hard reality of stardom, Jack Johnson was just not willing to work that hard.

'I wasn't sure it was really something I wanted to do and I didn't want to sign something that was going to be hard to get out of two months down the line,' Johnson would later recall in an interview with *Detours* Magazine. 'In most of the meetings, when I was talking to those people, they would have some ideas. It's not the fact that they liked the little bit of what they heard, but that they had some ideas on how they could market it and change it.'

Needless to say, Johnson left that meeting without a deal and the corporate suit mumbling unbelieving at the notion that people like Jack Johnson even existed. It would be a scenario that would play out several times with Johnson leaving with his integrity, purity and apparent lack of ambition intact.

So while Jack Johnson would much rather be surfing or doing nothing than doing business, there was a definite, albeit unorthodox, business mind at work behind the laidback demeanor. It was an unwavering insistence that he maintain complete control over his sound and his style. It was that insistence that had Johnson saying no to some mighty appealing offers from the majors until 2001 when he finally agreed to a deal with the then newly formed independent label, Enjoy Records...Or rather Enjoy agreed with Jack.

The deal, according to the equally harmonious Enjoy Records honcho

J.P. Plunier, allowed Johnson to have complete control of his songs, when he would record and, most importantly to the singer-songwriter, when he would tour. The watch word being if and when Johnson decided to do anything. Plunier would later laughingly acknowledge that it would be impossible to tell a kid who grew up on Pipeline that he could not surf.

This is how Jack Johnson does business. And so is this.

Jack Johnson was sitting in a Colorado restaurant called Illegal Pete's in 2001, chowing down on a monster burrito with a group of friends and band mates, when his cell phone rang. It was his manager Emmett Malloy with some good news.

Johnson, between bites of his burrito, listened as Malloy explained that Universal Records had expressed an interest in picking up his debut album, *Brushfire Fairytales*, for worldwide distribution. Malloy went on at length about what such a deal would mean in terms of getting his album into stores, raising his level of popularity and, yes, increasing his income. The wheels in Johnson's head began to turn.

Brushfire Fairytales had done amazingly well for a small independent release; selling an estimated 75,000 copies behind good word of mouth, a handful of supportive radio stations and a low-profile, no-budget touring regimen that regularly saw Johnson and his band playing in out of the way clubs for audiences that rarely numbered above a hundred. For Johnson, who had never had high expectations for a music career in the first place, this was a major accomplishment. He did not know if he was ready to sell out his self-perceived indie status and all important freedom for a bigger piece of the pie.

'They were offering an amount of money we never thought we'd get,' said Johnson in a recent interview with *Outside* Magazine. 'But I remember telling my friends, "Let's just say no."'

Barely holding back his laughter, Johnson relayed the rejection to Malloy who promptly hung up. Malloy was not upset with his charge. Matter of fact, Malloy knew implicitly how Johnson would react to the offer before it was even proffered. Because long before Malloy became his manager, he had been his surfing buddy, filmmaking associate and somebody who Johnson considered a friend.

In fact it was the latter trait that was the reason, rather than any knowledge of the music business, that led the singer to ask Malloy to act as, or more accurately play at, being his manager. Which is why Malloy knew exactly what to go back and tell the inquiring label.

Johnson returned to his burrito. Five minutes later his cell phone rang again. It was Malloy. Universal's offer had been doubled. Again Johnson said thanks but no thanks. In his mind, this all important business decision had turned into one big game and he was having a hell of a good time playing it.

Johnson could afford to play hardball. At the moment, he really did not care if he made it big in the world of popular music. He was having the time of his life travelling to small venues in a cramped mini-van, making a marginal living on the club circuit and being able to drop it all when the mood hit him to travel halfway around the world to catch a wave when the surf was high in places like Indonesia and Australia. Music was just a temporary side trip, a hobby to play at before doing whatever he felt like doing next.

Jack Johnson basically did not give a shit about being a star and that was a weapon the corporate world had no defense against nor could throw any amount of money at.

Johnson's ploy worked. Some months later, Universal approached Johnson a third time and finally agreed to his terms in the later stages of 2001.

'The third time they came to us and said, "You tell us what you want, you make up your own deal,"' said Johnson in a *Billboard* magazine interview. 'So we set things up in a way that we have a really independent situation. We turn in our records once they're finished; nobody ever sees or hears them until then.'

This is the way Jack Johnson does business and five years later it has made him a legitimate star. Albeit a fairly low profile one.

Johnson's third album, *In Between Dreams*, was released in March 2005 and went gold in a month. By June it had risen to number two on the *Billboard* charts and had sold more than a million copies in the US, which brought Johnson's total sales of his first three albums to well over four million.

Summer 2005 saw Johnson and his band embark on a three month cross country tour. But where previous tours saw Johnson and his mates packed like sardines into a mini-van whose windows did not always go up and down as they crisscrossed the country playing often sparsely attended club dates; these days Johnson and his band are travelling in relative style in eco-friendly buses to concert venues that have regularly seen the singer-songwriter ply his mellow trade in front of as many as 20,000 fans.

A concert DVD of an early 2005 performance in the US and a 2004 performance in Japan hit the shelves just in time for Christmas. A round of European concerts slated for early 2006 sold out three months before his appearance. Johnson had also become the darling of Hollywood when he contributed music and songs to the soundtrack of the big budget movie version of the classic children's book *Curious George*.

But what has not changed amid all the hoopla is the low key, self effacing way in which Johnson continues to go about his business. Jack Johnson is the same person he was before fame and fortune found him and, much like the mellow mix of folk, soul and reggae that has brought him his success, he looks at his success as almost an afterthought.

When he talks about touring, it's usually in the enthusiastic tones of the cool people, like Ben Harper and Neil Young, that he has gotten to meet. When he talks about recording, it's as simple as writing some words, jamming with some friends and having songs come out of it. Obviously it's a lot more complex than Johnson makes it out to be but Johnson is not the type to examine anything to the point where it gets too difficult.

Take stardom for instance.

'It's been an amazing series of events,' Johnson has said matter of factly of his rise to stardom in the *Daily Trojan*. 'I have always tried to let it flow. It sounds cheesy or overly Zen but I have always tried to go along with whatever happened naturally.'

And while humble may be a good gimmick in these egocentric times, there are plenty of people lining up to say that when it comes to humility, Jack Johnson is the real thing.

'He's just the mellowest guy in the world,' acknowledged long time friend Chris Mauro in a 2005 interview. 'He's very quiet and unassuming. When he meets somebody for the first time, he's really quite shy.'

Johnson's older brother Pete in a *Sports Illustrated* interview echoed those sentiments. 'I don't think Jack will ever get too big for himself. He's always been a sensitive guy.'

J.P. Plunier, who produced *Brushfire Fairytales* has, likewise, stated on many occasions that humble Jack Johnson is the real thing.

'It's impossible to be around Jack and not think he's just a genuine cat,' he told *Sports Illustrated*. 'He's just a kid who surfs. He's never wanted the limelight.'

Former professional surfer and longtime family friend, Corky Carroll, agreed with the notion that stardom had not changed Johnson during a 2005 interview. 'It looks to me that if any superstar has ever had his head on straight, it's Jack. He seems to be a solid family man and he cares about the planet.'

Johnson's 'aw shucks' demeanour was put to the test during the 2005 concert tour. The singer-songwriter had long ago developed an ease in performing that allowed him to turn audiences of 5000 or more into intimate, living room gatherings. But the laidback mystique of earlier, more intimate tours had been overtaken by something approaching near Beatles-like mania that often came as an unexpected surprise for the shy troubadour.

He smiled good naturedly one night when a fan in the front row blew marijuana smoke in his face. On another, he was downright embarrassed when a woman's panties came sailing out of the audience and landed at his feet. Likewise, his face turned several shades of red when, on another night, a bra flew out of the audience and narrowly missed his head. Finally the 2005 concert trail was regularly marked by nubile young beach babes showing their appreciation by baring their breasts.

Johnson's wife Kim, who these days often goes on the road with her husband and their two-year-old son Moe in tow, has witnessed these concert highjinks first hand but has no fear of losing her husband to the excesses of stardom.

'I suppose I might be concerned if he started to like all the attention,' she has said in *Outside* magazine, 'but he doesn't.'

Mauro supported the notion that Johnson is very much a family man even as the perks of stardom and celebrity swirl around him.

'His wife is the number one person in his life. When he's backstage, you can usually find him in some out of the way corner, sitting with Kim or playing with his son Moe. He's comfortable on stage and he's comfortable with the attention. But he's not into being a rock star. He goes on stage, does his thing and then goes home.'

An urban legend of sorts has popped up in the Santa Barbara Ca. Area where Johnson lived for several years before relocating to Oahu, Hawaii. Johnson reportedly walked into a local record shop and bought forty copies of *Brushfire Fairytales* and walked out without being recognized.

The truth is that, before stardom tapped him on the shoulder, he quite easily walked among us without being recognized. Even today, in certain situations, Jack Johnson can become invisible.

Because Jack Johnson looks every inch a real person.

His build is muscular in a lean sort of way. There are no tattoos or piercings. The scars on his face from a long ago surfing accident radiate character rather than disfigurement. His greenish eyes project a soft and probing nature. The close cropped cut or often shaved head he favours mirrors a tribal simplicity. Put a uniform on him and he could pass as a poster boy for the marines. However, in his world, T-shirts, jeans, sandals and shorts are his wardrobe of choice.

The person? Jack Johnson is just so goddamned likeable! He'll talk to anybody about anything at any time. He gives the impression of some-body who has just stumbled into this three ring circus and is not quite sure how he got here.

Does he get angry? Sure. But in his world anger rarely rises above the level of mild annoyance and frustration. Take the time somebody acci-dentally dropped and damaged a favourite guitar. He got mildly annoyed for a few minutes and then had the guitar repaired. Simple as that.

But all of this would mean nothing if it were not for the fact that Jack Johnson had something to offer, business bottom line, his music. A sim-plistic musical contract that has struck a totally escapist chord in people too caught up in the rigours of daily life to ever imagine waves, sandy beaches and swaying palms in their world. We've signed the contract and, in return, we get songs like 'Bubble Toes', a funny, loving ode to Johnson's wife, 'Sitting, Waiting, Wishing', a smooth ode to love lost and found and the amusingly funky 'F Stop Blues' which was written during a bout of sea sickness.

The songs? Never as challenging as they are playful and heartfelt. His medium of expression is acoustic, a sincere soulful white man voice, marked by imperfections and backed by simple rhythm and percussion. Never a hint of electric and only mildly rocking. It is a musical formula that Johnson sees no reason to change and makes no apologies for.

The looseness of the Jack Johnson musical experience, with its starts, stops, between song patter that often goes nowhere but is always good for a laugh, is a throwback to a non-conformist, populist style of performing that, doubtless, had its roots in the freewheeling sixties. And a big reason for Johnson's unpolished live bent is the fact that, almost from the beginning, there has been a no rehearsal edict in place

'It's funnier that way,' he once said in a *Synthesis* magazine interview. 'When you practice too much, it becomes like a performance instead of a party. What we are playing is feel good music. Our whole thing is providing a party.'

The Jack Johnson party bus shows no signs of slowing down. However Johnson seems aware of the fleeting nature of pop stardom and, while his music appears geared for the long haul, in his mind he is prepared for the end if and when it comes.

He has indicated that he'd like to take some time off and return to his first love, documentary filmmaking. And, in conversation with Mauro and others, he has stated that he would not let celebrity ever become a drag on his personal life or his freedom. Because that is how Jack Johnson does business and business is never far from a wave and a long board.

As if to drive that point home, Johnson has often explained that his music was like a wave and when the time came to kick out from this wave, he would.

02

Paradise Found: Pre Jack

For as far back in time as men took to the sea in search of fame, fortune and adventure, they were known as Watermen.

There was no literal translation of the word and it has gone by different names in different languages over the centuries in large and small countries all over the world. But if you were to put the words 'fearless' and 'experimentation' next to the word Waterman, you would have a fair definition.

Watermen did not move according to society's expectations. They were not easily tied down. Their soul and reason for being was just over the next wave or out beyond the far horizon. To be a Waterman in any time in earth's history was to be something special.

Coming out of World War II and into the safe, bland, conformist Eisenhower years, there was a genuine shortage of Watermen or, for that matter, any kind of free spirits abroad in America in the 50s. The beats had dug in in San Francisco and had made it their home. The most progressive writers and artists of the day had long since packed their bags and left for Europe. It would be nearly 20 years before anyone would use the word 'hippie' as a noun.

And then there was Jeff Johnson, wiling away his days shooting the curl on the surf of Manhattan Beach, California, one of a cluster of Southern California beach towns that formed the South Bay which lay in quiet defiance of the planes that regularly zipped in and out of nearby Los Angeles International Airport. He was somebody who instinctively embodied the Waterman credo without ever having heard the word.

'My dad is the kind of character you would read books about,' Johnson would tell *The Independent*. 'He's one of those guys that I would never be able to be as cool as. He wasn't a hipster so much as he was a sailor. He was like somebody out of a Steinbeck story.'

Jeff Johnson was born in 1944. Jeff was a normal, inquisitive child who, even at a young age, was prone to flights of imagination and a natural dreamer. His parents were of a fairly liberal persuasion and those traits were passed on to their son. Johnson gravitated toward the wonders of nature and the great outdoors at an early age. He was introduced to the water as a very young boy and immediately formed a bond with it; a psychic-spiritual connection that, in later years, would anchor him to the sand and surf.

Jeff had gravitated quite naturally to surfing. There was something in the primal challenge of man verses nature and the just plain 'cool' of riding down the crest of a mountainous wave that appealed to him. By the time he reached his teens, he could be found on the water almost everyday, testing himself when the surf was high. There was a style and ease to Jeff Johnson the surfer.

There was nary a hint of pretense in his make-up. He did not do things for effect. Jeff Johnson did not have to do anything to be cool. He was just quite naturally that way.

The professional surf scene was very much in its infancy in the 50s in the United States at that point. And unlike the almost reverential popularity of the sport in most of the rest of the world, those who did surf in America, whether professional or amateur, were often looked upon as radical undesirables. Jeff heard the comments but he did not think too deeply about things like that. All he knew was the lure of the sea and an imagination fired with adventure in far off places.

Patti Johnson was cut from the same kind of cloth. The child of a liberal, socially and spiritually aware family, Patti found her early years immersed in the joys of books and art. She was not a surfer. But, like Jeff, she had an innate curiosity about the surf and what lay beyond the breakers. The two seemed destined to cross paths and they did...Very early on in their lives.

Jeff and Patti met in the first grade. They became good friends and remained so until the nature of the relationship became a bit more serious in junior high school. They dated for a while but then drifted apart. But the pair reunited in their senior year of high school in 1961.

What had broken them up years earlier had all but been forgotten. What they found was that their suddenly rekindled attraction to each other had been fueled by their love for the ocean and a simpler way of life. This bond drew them closer together and eventually became true love.

Jeff and Patti married shortly after graduating from high school. Their first child, a son named Trent, was born in 1965. There's was an idyllic existence. The couple had settled in the South Bay area. Jeff supported his family on a modest income from various jobs and, of course, surfed every chance he'd get. Patti was quite content to stay home and be a traditional housewife and mother.

Jeff had given thought to trying to make a living on the professional surfing circuit. Those who had seen him on the waves had often commented that he had an aggressive style that was ideally suited for the pro circuit. But while he craved the adventure and the opportunity to travel the world that surfing offered, there was something about surfing as a moneymaking venture that turned him off to that notion for even at a fairly young age, Jeff had come to savour the purity of things. Also his sense of responsibility to Patti and his concept of family was strong and the time he would have to be away from his family too great for Jeff to take those thoughts too seriously.

But in his early 20s Jeff once again began to dream the impossible dream.

Jeff read the magazines, saw the movies and had his ear to the ground when it came to all things connected to the surfing lifestyle, a sense of peace and natural living that had a strong attraction. It seemed like more and more, he had begun hearing the stories from surfers who had gone to Hawaii and, in particular, the island of Oahu. Stories about monster waves that broke at Pipeline and the laidback lifestyle that permeated the island and its ways. Jeff conjured up a picture in his head of Oahu as a modern day Garden Of Eden where nobody and nothing was in a hurry. And he liked what he saw.

Jeff's spirit of adventure was once again fueled by those tales. He would daydream of being there. The idea of responsibility and normalcy had been washed away by the spirit of the Waterman.

One night over dinner Jeff matter of factly announced that they were going to move to Oahu. The move, supported by Patti who, by this time, had gotten used to her husband's impulsiveness and, truth be known, loved the idea of moving to a far off place, seemed simple enough. But if it had been simple, it would not have been Jeff.

Jeff had been taking sailing lessons for the past few months and had gotten fairly adept at handling the family's pride and joy, a 25 foot long sloop. And so, rather than simply fly to the islands, he decided to sail the sloop alone to Oahu and send for his wife and son once he established himself on the island. Going to Oahu with little sailing experience and no prospects seemed rash but Jeff, with the spirit of the Waterman flowing through his veins, saw this adventure into the unknown differently.

'I felt a long trip like that would be the best way to figure it all out,' he said in a *Surfer* magazine article.

So on a somewhat overcast Southern California morning, his sails billowing to catch the wind, Jeff set out into the Pacific. As he looked back on the last shadows of land disappearing beneath the horizon, Jeff reasoned that he had enough food and water to get him to Oahu and whatever would happen next. Jeff looked forward. Oahu was in his future.

Things went well for the first few days. Jeff took to the role of sailor and seemed more than up to the task of guiding his vessel into the teeth of any friendly wind and keeping the sloop on a steady, outward bound course. The slightly choppy water was never threatening. When not attending to sailing duties, Jeff would lapse into deep thought. He would gaze out onto an endless stretch of the Pacific, thinking about his wife and child and, in a more abstract way, dream of riding big surf and how they would live and thrive in the Hawaii of his dreams.

The dream became a nightmare a week into his voyage when the spreader on the sloop's mast broke, making it literally impossible for Jeff to sail the boat. Jeff was left bobbing up and down in the middle of the ocean with the prospect of rations running out, bad weather a lingering possibility and land nowhere in sight. But luck had not deserted him.

A passing boat happened by, saw Jeff's predicament and pulled up alongside him. It was at that point that Jeff learned firsthand about the code of the sea. One of the crewmen hopped on board the sloop and offered to help Jeff fix the spreader. The other boat moved on with the agreement that the spreader would be quickly fixed and the sloop would catch up with the boat and redeposit the crewman.

Unfortunately the job took longer than expected and, by the time the two men had fixed the spreader, the other boat was already more than a day ahead of them. With sails up, Jeff and his newfound friend gave chase.

Adding to Jeff's troubled odyssey was the fact that there was only enough food on board for one. With two men now eating, the rations were quickly running low. But their luck continued to hold as a school of Mahi Mahi had taken a liking to the sloop and had been swimming along underneath its hull. Each day, Jeff and his fellow sailor would drop a line into the ocean and haul a good sized fish on board, which they would then cook and eat. This routine would go on for ten days when, with a full week left before they hit dry land, they ran out of matches. Jeff would often recall how unpleasant it was for that week, trying to eat the fish raw.

Jeff finally landed on Oahu and soon was reunited with Patti and Trent. The family's first home was a tiny house in the small town of Hauula on the east side of Oahu. There was a gradual feeling out process as Jeff and his family integrated themselves into the largely Hawaiian and Samoan population. But they were also happy to discover that Oahu had already come to be the equivalent of San Francisco's Haight-Ashbury, a place where many Americans had come for many reasons.

'When he (Jeff) first came to Oahu, the North Shore was inhabited by fishermen, carpenters, surfers and working-class people,' reflected Johnson in an *Independent* interview. 'My parents didn't stand out because there were all these other eccentrics about the place also trying to get away from mainstream America and coming here to dodge the draft.'

Pro surfer Corky Carroll, who would bond with the Johnson family on his many surfing trips to the island, recalled that the Johnsons had the perfect mindset for fitting into island life. 'They were a tight family who were totally into the lifestyle and spirit of the island. They were good people and easy to be around.'

It was paradise but at least at the beginning it was paradise with a price. From the moment the Johnson's set down roots on the island, they were literally living hand to mouth.

The diet of fish that had enabled Jeff to make it to Oahu became their principle diet and hinged largely on Jeff's skills as a fisherman. If something needed to be repaired, Jeff either repaired it or it stayed broken. Jeff, an instinctive hustler in the good sense of the word, was always finding ways to put food on the table and a few dollars in their pocket.

Jeff worked for a time as a boat builder, doing well enough that the Johnson family (now grown to four with the birth of their second son Peter in 1968) moved to their long coveted North Shore digs, a small nondescript house just minutes from Ehukai Beach Park and approximately 100 yards to Pipeline and some of the biggest waves on the planet.

Jeff continued to find work as a boat builder and, with the acquaintance of islander Jose Angel, would supplement the family income by diving for fish, turtles, coral and other deep sea treasures he would then sell to local restaurants and tourist stands.

When not working, Jeff would race off to Pipeline to test his mettle against the surf. An old school, long board surfer with an instinctive sense of courage when attacking the waves, Jeff quickly earned a reputation as one of the better surfers around and would, over the years, surf in his fair share of pro tournaments held on the island.

But the island of Oahu was as far as Jeff was willing to take any professional aspirations. The grounded nature that had served him well on the mainland was continuing. The taste of the surfing life was all he needed. There was no need to follow the sun.

Because Jeff and Patti Johnson had truly found paradise.

Jeff moved up from boat building to construction work and would later get his contractor's license which finally brought the family's financial situation into stability for the first time. Despite the influx of money, the Johnson's remained true to the island way of life. They need only look out the front door of their modest home, at the waves tumbling in on the beach to know in their hearts that they had everything they needed.

Not that the Johnson family did not indulge the occasional whim. There near constant diet of fish that had sustained them since arriving at Oahu was now supplemented by such luxuries as beef and chicken. And Patti has always remembered the day that the family paid cash for her very own car, a big, lumbering and very eccentric Cadillac.

That the car would not go into reverse went largely unnoticed. It was a symbolic reflection to a family lifestyle that was nothing if not unorthodox. The Johnson family was moving on in paradise as Patti went into labour for the third time.

03

Growing Up Wet

Jack Hody Johnson was born on May 18, 1975.

For those present at the birth, it was almost a Zen-like experience. Mixed in with the cries of the newborn were the subtle, constant sounds of Hawaii wafting up gently in the background. The thundering of surf as it crashed into white foam on the shore. The soft sound of wind whipping easily through swaying palms. It would be almost too poetic to think that the forces of nature were welcoming one of their own into the world.

But from the moment Jack Johnson opened his eyes for the first time and took in the world around him, one could sense a closeness with his environment. He would later recall a sense of psychic connection with the lifestyle of sun, surf and the simple pleasures that had become a literal island paradise created by Jeff and Patti Johnson on a stretch of Oahu beach that looked out over Hawaii's famous, gently breaking Pupukea surf...

Johnson has always proclaimed himself a believer in the spirituality of nature and has often attempted to come to grips with those early child-hood memories and although he concedes that said memories are hazy, they were most definitely there.

'It's weird,' Johnson said in an interview with *Surfing Vancouver Island*. 'Since before I really had memories, I had images in my head of riding down waves, watching the water go by, just abstract memories.'

Memories that were fuelled by the fact that Oahu's legendary Pipeline and its 15 foot waves that would, unexpectedly, go from left to right breaks, was closer to the Johnson home than their mailbox, some 200 yards down the beach.

'We lived on the beach, right in front of Pipeline,' said Johnson in an *Outside Online* interview. 'When the waves got gigantic, the crashing would rumble our windows at night.'

Where there was surf, there were surf riders, the young men who would venture out in all kinds of weather to challenge the monster waves. Surfing was a tradition on the islands that went back hundreds of years and was the backbone of the culture that had thrived on Oahu.

It was an unwritten code on the shore that local children would begin their assault on the Pipeline just as soon as they could walk. In the case of Jeff and Patti Johnson the attitude was particularly strong. Their two eldest sons, Trent and Peter, were on boards shortly after taking their first steps and, under their parent's guidance, would develop into two of the more competitive surfers on the island.

With their third child, things would not be different.

At age four, at a time when most youngsters are asking for their first bike, Johnson was being introduced to the wonders of the waves and the feel of the long board. The elder Johnson had his son kneel down on the front of his board on that first day and calmly paddled out to meet the first set of good sized waves. There was excitement and nervousness on the boy's face as water lapped up onto the board and against his body. But with his father's soothing, encouraging words, Johnson was not afraid. On father and son's very first ride, an unexpected slap of wave upended the board and pitched the youngster into the water. But rather than be traumatised, Johnson emerged from the water exhilarated as he shook the water from his face and was ready to go out again.

Years later, Johnson would lovingly recall how his father would grab him up and head out on the water at the first sign of surf.

Ever the cautious parent, Jeff would initially only take his son out on what would be considered small wave days. This rite of passage saw the youngster sitting on his knees on the front of the board, taking in the spray and smiling the smile of a child experiencing something truly amazing at a very young age. Surfing being the family affair that it was, Johnson's older brothers would also take turns introducing him to the wonders of the sea and surf.

The next step was for Jack to get his own board.

'I was five years old when I got my first surfboard,' recalled Johnson years later in an interview with *The Independent*. 'It (surfing) became so ingrained in who I am and how I find balance in my life. My dad raised us in the ocean. It became a sort of church for us. It's where we would go to find family unity.'

The Johnson family equation of water plus togetherness equals unity ran beyond just surfing to the time-honoured Waterman influence of sailing. Which, Johnson recalled in a *Honolulu Weekly* article, infused him with moral and spiritual values that would last a lifetime.

'My dad spent a good deal of his life on boats,' said Johnson, 'and he shared that with me. My best memories of childhood are of being out on a Hawaiian canoe with my dad.'

Johnson recalled in the same interview that a yearly highlight would be the canoe trips across the ocean to the island of Maui. 'It was the most exhilarating, rewarding experience and we had very little in the way of supplies. I learned from my dad that when you're living on a boat, you keep it simple and you keep your possessions at a level where you only use what you need.'

For the Johnson family, it was a joyous and symbolic passing of the torch to the next generation of wave riders. And it was a torch being threatened by the winds of change that were pushing the old ways aside in the name of progress.

Barely two decades removed from statehood, Hawaii was making its way into the modern age. Long the destination of only a select circle of super rich, the lush, tropical islands had blossomed into a glitzy tourist mecca. Modern high rise hotels and trendy, upscale restaurants had become the norm in big cities like Honolulu. The traditional luau and ceremonial hula dance were now simply parts of the package.

It was only on the outer fringes of the more seaward islands, down small, dusty and often precarious roads that a mixture of Hawaiians and a smattering of expatriates from other shores were attempting to keep the past alive amid small clusters of huts and houses built of nature's raw materials and setting close by the sea.

Jack Johnson was born old school; a living breathing by-product of those ancient ways. Johnson, much like his father, was a free spirit who craved the simple, natural pleasures that went beyond money and all things material. In later years, Johnson's brothers would often describe his demeanour as almost Ghandi-like. 'Most of the time, he was the one teaching Pete and I how to behave,' recalled Trent in a *Surfer* magazine profile.

Jack Johnson was learning to live in Eden and one need only look to his roots to discover the reason why.

'My dad led a simple life,' Johnson told the *Chicago Tribune*. 'Looking at him made me realise that you don't need a lot to be happy.'

Johnson would often recall of those years that he developed a near spiritual bond with his homeland. 'When I was a kid it was real country,' he told the *Strand*. 'Dirt roads, a lot of space, a lot of coconut trees and really good waves. It's a real pretty spot and everybody has a lot of space.'

Johnson's early years were marked by an ease and maturity well beyond his years. Those around him remember Johnson being a polite child and one who would immediately offer a handshake when meeting somebody for the first time. Patti Johnson would acknowledge that it had made some of their friends uncomfortable because they had not immediately responded to the young Johnson's overtures. He would look a person straight in the eye when talking to them and would listen intently. Johnson was also possessed of an innate sense of humour, regardless of whether a joke was being played on him or the roles were reversed.

On one such occasion his older brother Pete had convinced his younger brother that the only way to deal with a cut on his foot was to amputate the foot, and that Johnson would have to do it. The younger brother went in the house, came back with a butcher's knife and began sawing on his brother's ankle before Pete finally let him off the hook. Johnson's response was to be upset because he felt he had not done it right.

Johnson began his formal education in 1980 at Sunset Elementary School. A naturally bright and inquisitive child with an unexpectedly good aptitude for numbers, Johnson was moved along quite rapidly, often finding himself among the more advanced students in the school.

'I keep hearing the story that I was never late the entire seven years I was at Sunset,' he recalled in a *Honolulu Weekly* interview, 'and it's probably true. I was a little worrywart when it came to things like that. I was also kind of a nerd. But I had fun with school. I was never one of those guys who dreaded school.'

Almost from day one, Johnson, as his brothers had before him, found himself a minority, the rare white face among a primarily Hawaiian and Samoan student body. During his early school years, he would learn that 'Haole' was often the equivalent of 'Nigger'. But while there were the occasional dust ups, Johnson's good humour, laidback nature and the ability to make everybody around him feel like his best friend usually won the day.

While he thrived in academic surroundings, school was often an after-thought, something that took up the time when he was not surfing. The surfing gods had not made it easy for Johnson and his surfing buddies. During the school year, the waves at Pipeline broke big and majestic. When school was out, the water was flat and calm. During such holidays, Johnson and his friends would often jump into an outrigger and paddle to the other side of the island where the waves would be at their best. When school was in session, they would resort to a different schedule.

One that was often aided and abetted by Johnson's mother's liberal at-titude; Johnson would always joke about the fact that, when the surf was good on a school day, 'she would always let me stay home.'

Typically, Johnson and his brothers would be up at dawn and race out the sliding glass door of their home to grab a few waves before leaving for school. After school, they would surf until dinner and, later, would often be found sitting on the shoreline, watching the sun set over the few remaining surfers who were attempting a last ride.

As a child, the lure and mystique of the surfing lifestyle had already planted itself deep in the young boy's psyche.

'All I ever dreamed of was being a pro surfer,' he would recall years later in several publications including *Rolling Stone*. 'For me, it's like I was de-tatched from the world when I was in the ocean. It was like flying, float-ing and harnessing the energy that comes from the ocean. I loved those feelings. Surfing is all any kid who grows up here wants to be.'

Corky Carroll, who by this time was a regular visitor to Oahu and had become fast friends with the Johnson family, recalled in a 2005 interview that when it came to surfing, the young Johnson already had the eye of the tiger. 'He was always surfing. Jack seemed much like every other young dude, growing up surfing on the world's most powerful beach. He was really jazzed all the time.'

Johnson's dream of a surfing life was fuelled by the up close and per-sonal contact he had with the many pro surfers who came to Oahu on a regular basis to test their mettle against the North Shore. Jeff and Patti always had an open door policy when it came to visitors and so it was not uncommon for Johnson to come home from school to find such legendary surfers as Gerry Lopez, Derek Ho and Laird Hamilton sitting on his parent's front porch, enjoying a brew, storing their surfboards in the Johnson's shed and enjoying Patti Johnson's specialty, Shoyu Chicken.

Johnson's 10th birthday was an important one in the life of the Johnson family. Jeff had managed to scrape together enough money for the family to move to a bigger house. That bigger move meant moving two hundred yards down the street to a home that now literally had Pipeline lapping at their front porch.

Johnson has looked back at those formative years and admitted to being a starstruck kid when he would see the likes of Rabbit Bartholomew, Tom Curren and Mark Occhilupo walking down the street or grabbing a slice at the local pizza parlour.

'It was really a small neighbourhood and so I'd always see them cruising around,' he said in a *Surfing Vancouver Island* interview. 'I'd see these guys in the front yard a lot before I'd see them in the surf magazines. I was like any other surf kid growing up. Tom Curren was like God to me and then you'd get to see God walking around the street or hanging out in the park by your house. It was amazing.'

But while awe-struck when around the much older pros, Johnson did have an ego when it came to his own surfing skills. He knew he did not come close to measuring up to the pros but he was quietly cocksure when it came to his skills relative to non pros his age. Consequently, his competitive juices were up the summer he turned 12 when a 15-year-old pro on the rise named Kelly Slater began hanging out at Oahu and testing the Pipeline.

'Before I even knew Kelly, I remember that he would come over and surf the sandbars,' Johnson said with no small amount of ego in his voice in Kelly Slater's autobiography. 'My friends and I were the up and coming kids from Hawaii who were all riding the big surf. But eventually he submerged himself in our group and would get to the level of all the crazy kids on the North Shore.'

Their respective competitive, free-spirited natures soon brought Johnson and Slater together in a friendship that continues to this day. The year Johnson met Slater was also the year when Donovan Frankenreiter, a surfing phenomenon at the ripe old age of 13, came to Hawaii to get his surf legs at Oahu. Frankenreiter rented a tiny room above the Johnson family garage during that initial visit and formed a similar bond with the young boy. In Jack Johnson's world, friendship was as simple as riding a wave.

By the time Johnson turned 13, he had effectively worked himself into the clique that made Pipeline their home away from home. And as he recalled, the order of Pipeline was something you had to earn.

'I started going out on bigger days and we'd just sit on the shoulder and just watch,' he said to *Ninemsn*. 'We'd spend hours out there just watching and then slowly you'd ease out a little closer to the line-up. There's a pecking order that's real crazy. As a kid, you watch and watch and one day you end up on the peak, a good one comes through and everybody makes sure you get that one. So by the time you're 15 or 16 you start getting waves and by the time you're 17 or 18 you start being a little punk and taking over the peak and pushing the older guys off. It's a cycle that happens every few years.'

Johnson is at a loss to remember the first time he caught a wave but he couched the memory of an early, memorable ride in very Zen-like terms that, from an early age, mirrored his attitude toward surfing and the sea.

In explaining the experience to others, the youngster would paint a picture of gliding down a tube, looking out of it at the world around him and seeing it as a microcosm of life. He saw it as the most primal of spiritual challenges; physically and mentally ducking, dodging and improvising in a timeless battle with the forces of nature that had ingrained itself deeply on his psyche and outlook on life.

By day, Johnson and his growing circle of surf locals and selected outsiders, a wave mafia if you will which by this time included Kelly Slater and superstars in the making Rob Machado and Shane Dorian, would amuse themselves on North Shore with surf challenges like 'You Won't Go' and 'The Back Door Paddle Out Contest.' At night, they would gather at impromptu parties at somebody's house or at a beach location where, inevitably, somebody in the crowd, usually their neighbour Skill Johnson (no relation) or family friend Peff Eick, would produce an acoustic guitar, pluck a few rudimentary chords and start to sing.

Like everything else along the Hawaiian landscape, the music rarely rose above a mellow sigh.

Music in Hawaii had long been a mixmaster of styles and attitudes. In the big cities and more touristy areas, Don Ho and his mixture of traditional island rhythms and glossy, vapid pop (typified by Ho's signature tune 'Tiny Bubbles') was the most well known musical form. But get out into the countryside or into the smattering of hipper clubs and gatherings and it was a hybrid of time honoured Hawaiian and Reggae elements called Jawaiian that attracted a young but no less mellow following.

Finally, when people gathered informally to party like Johnson and his friends, it was raw, unpolished mellow folk or acoustic takes on the big hits of the day that were most in keeping with the laidback nature of island life. It was on nights like this that Johnson sat mesmerized as he took in the good vibes of the quiet music.

But Johnson recalled in a *Los Angeles City Beat* that his introduction to music came at a relatively early age and largely consisted of traditional Hawaiian music. 'My parents listened to it all the time. Stuff like Gabby Pahinui and a lot of slack key music. I'd always hear it in the house. That mellow style definitely sunk in.'

However, as he got older, Johnson would find musical enlightenment in island interpretations of popular hits.

'The music I got turned onto was by friends of my dad's who could play guitar or ukulele,' Johnson reflected in an *Outside Online* feature. 'They would sit around for hours playing songs by Bob Marley, Cat Stevens or The Beatles.'

It was in this setting that Johnson discovered a landlocked counter to his surfing life. Something to be savoured in its simplicity. Something that would leave a mark in Jack Johnson's creative psyche.

Like most kids, Johnson learned about popular music from his brother's hand-me-downs; the latest albums by Kiss, Black Sabbath, Queen, Jimi Hendrix, Devo and Men At Work which he wore to scratchy bare vinyl on a child's plastic record player. The hippest radio station in Hawaii, KUTH, a staple on rides to and from school, indoctrinated Johnson in the joys of such cutting edge new wave bands as Radiohead, Fugazi, Minor Threat, Suicidal Tendencies and Bad Religion.

His liberal parents took a very young Johnson to his very first concert by the band Devo. His first concert without his parents was a Ziggy Marley show which opened the youngsters' ears to the power of reggae.

However it was the ease and spontaneity of the informal beach jams that fascinated and finally inspired Johnson, at age 14, to pick up a guitar and learn how to play.

Borrowing an old, beat up acoustic guitar from a friend, the teenager would spend his nights patiently picking out chords in an attempt to master the basics. As friends often do, Frankenreiter was quick to emulate Johnson's musical aspirations and the pair would often get together to practice. Another friend Cale Tilley soon joined in on the informal practice sessions.

Johnson's immediate goal was to learn how to play a passable version of Van Morrison's 'Brown Eyed Girl'. The first songs he would actually learn how to play were Metallica's 'One' and Cat Steven's 'Father And Son'. After months of practice, he would add songs by The Beatles, Bob Marley and Jimmy Buffet to a set that he would eventually play in front of others.

At a time when most teens dream about being rock stars, Johnson was a bit more pragmatic when it came to any musical ambitions. For him, it was a hobby, something to do at night or when the surf was not high. He was not learning guitar so he could be a star. He was learning guitar so he could hold his own at the sing-a-longs on his parent's front porch.

Carroll, who also played guitar, remembered that he would often take out his guitar when visiting the Johnsons and it seemed that on those occasions Johnson was always there. 'I used to see Jack on his front porch with a guitar in his hand but, honestly, I don't think I ever gave it much thought. I don't think I can ever remember hearing him play.'

Those privy to the first, informal concerts by Johnson confirmed that there was a sense of laidback, almost strident passion in the way he sang. His abilities with the guitar were basic. It never appeared that Johnson was engaging in anything but a good natured lark with no serious intent. In fact, Johnson was the first to jokingly acknowledge that he had no interest in being a rock star.

'I had no plans ever to do music besides goofing off and jamming with friends,' he has said in *Interview* magazine. 'It was a total goof to me. I never even took any lessons.'

Johnson's musical education continued to expand. At age 15, Damien Lovelock, the lead singer of the Australian punk rock band Celibate Rifles, rented the house right next door to the Johnsons'. He was on a working vacation, writing songs for a solo album but proved accommodating to the visits by Johnson who was thrilled at the idea of having an actual rock star living next door.

'I thought he was pretty cool,' Johnson recalled in a *Los Angeles City Beat* interview. 'He turned me on to Taj Mahal, Robert Johnson and all these blues guys. I was probably giving the music more of a chance at that point only because I thought he was so cool.'

It was at this juncture that Johnson began to make the connection between surf and music.

'When I was a kid, I used to watch a lot of different surf films and there would always be some kind of music in the background. There would be certain parts of films that I would rewind over and over again because I would see certain surfers and want to be like them. There might be a TSOL or Social Distortion song in the soundtrack of that part of the film and the song would get stuck in my head from watching it so many times.'

By his mid-teens Johnson had already decided that he was not interested in becoming a professional surfer which, at the time, was the de facto option for any island kid with a modicum of talent. He could see the coming of the new age of professional surfing as a big time sport complete with corporate sponsorship, big money and the rigours of a professional life. He saw those things as sucking all the joy he felt for the sport out of him.

'I would have made a good run at it,' recalled Johnson in a *City Paper* interview. 'But I struggled with thinking about it as a business. I wanted it to be more of a lifestyle than work.'

While he would tell anyone who would listen that he was only into surfing for the kicks, there was a consensus among those who had seen him ride that there was pro potential in Johnson's future if he chose to go that route.

'He doesn't abuse a wave, he dances with it,' said long-time surfing buddy Rob Machado in *Sports Illustrated* magazine. 'Watching him surf is beautiful.'

Growing up on the North Shore of Oahu was not all fun and games. For as far back as he could remember, Johnson recalled home 'as a crazy place, kind of like the Wild West'. The crime rate was high and the policing of the area was sporadic at best. Johnson would often relate that he was taught at an early age to settle his own problems whenever possible.

Johnson is not remembered as a fighter by those who knew him. But, by the time he turned 15, he had learned the formula for survival...which was to be humble but, more importantly, to be a standup guy.

Those attributes came in particularly handy when Johnson entered Oahu's notoriously tough Kahuku High School. Kahuku, made up largely of Hawaiian and Samoan students, did not always take kindly to the Haole (white kids) in the school. In fact the school was well known for its annual 'Beat Up A Haole Day' celebration. Johnson was able to navigate this minefield. His rep as a surfer carried some weight. So, to a much lesser degree, did his budding musicianship. But it was his ability to be tough when he had to be and as good as his word at all times that allowed him to survive his high school years.

And while never what anyone would consider a troublemaker, Johnson, in his high school years, could be a bit of a smart alec; especially when it came to balancing schooling and surfing.

'My friend, Adam Lerner, and I had it down to a science,' he said in *Honolulu Weekly*. 'He used to come and knock on my door anytime there were some decent waves and we'd go surf. We had it all mathematically figured out. We knew exactly when we had to get into the water, when we had to get out, one minute to shower and grab some toast, jump into the car and still get to school on time. Of course on time to us meant after the first bell and before the tardy bell. Sometimes we'd have to sweet talk our way out of trouble.'

But while there were occasional brushes with rebellion, the Johnson kids and Jack in particular were not close to being juvenile delinquents and that can be traced back to the liberal upbringing they had at the hands of their very liberal parents who, with the 60s hippie ethic very much ingrained in them, had a live-and-let-live attitude about what their children did.

'I never had that period of rebellion because my parents never gave me a reason to have one,' he told *The Independent*. 'They walked that line between letting us experiment with things while making sure that we were never idiots. They were like, "Look, we know you're going to parties and stuff but always be respectful and if you need a ride home, just call us and we'll come and get you rather than having you drive around drunk."'

With his parents' blessing, Johnson's interest in music continued to take in a more wide-ranging world. Punk, speed metal and hardcore music were beginning to become more of an influence. But musically, Johnson recalled leading a double life.

'We'd play all these hardcore punk records in the garage at my brother's house,' he told a *Los Angeles Times* reporter. 'Then quietly, at night, I'd learn how to play Cat Stevens, Neil Young and Jimmy Buffet.'

Johnson's passion for punk music became slightly more serious shortly after his sixteenth birthday when his always supportive parents bought him an electric guitar and a distortion pedal and encouraged him to make some noise. With some like-minded friends, he formed a punk rock band called Limber Chicken. Loud and obnoxious in a goofy sort of way: 'Being in a punk band was great because nobody had to be that good. You just needed a lot of energy.'

Limber Chicken spent most of their brief existence holed up in available garages, belting out punk rock favourites and a few Jack Johnson-penned originals. Limber Chicken was committed to posterity via a primitive four-track recording. Johnson would laugh years later when he recalled his mother's reaction to the recording.

'She would say, "It sounds so good honey,"' he recalled in a *Rolling Stone* interview. 'We'd be screaming our heads off and she would say how nice our voices sounded.'

Limber Chicken, whose members performed dressed in very unpunk-like flip flops and Hawaiian shorts, would play only three scattered gigs at area house parties before packing it in. Johnson's stage presence, exaggerated rock star poses and grimacing facial contortions, was all for laughs and in keeping with the non-serious nature of the band. It was during his stint with Limber Chicken, that Johnson first began to deal with the idea of being front and centre.

'Even though I wrote most of the songs we played, another guy in the band sang them,' he admitted in a *Launch* magazine interview. 'I never took singing lessons and, at that point, I didn't feel comfortable being the singer.'

Johnson's creative talents were also beginning to show an artistic side. Always a fairly good pencil artist, Johnson, at the suggestion of his older brother Trent and a book of paintings by Salvador Dali, began to paint.

'I really got into surrealism,' he said in a *Honolulu Weekly* article. 'For me, it's sort of an escape, just like surfing. I would just start out with a blank page and a pen and not really know what I was going to create.'

Johnson's surfing skills eventually came to the attention of Quicksilver, one of the major sponsorship players on the burgeoning pro circuit. The same year Limber Chicken began to play out, Quicksilver signed Johnson to his first professional contract; a $200 a month stipend that allowed him to compete in professional tournaments in Hawaii.

In spite of his misgivings about turning surfing into a business Johnson enjoyed being a pro and the pocket change supplied by Quicksilver did not hurt either. And although he would surf almost exclusively in Oahu during his tenure as a pro, primarily in Pipe Masters trial events and in a handful of Pro-Am contests, in the back of his mind Johnson entertained thoughts of using the pro circuit as a way to see the rest of the world. But those thoughts quickly lost out to the security of the island and home.

He loved Oahu and the Hawaiian lifestyle (as well as the occasional summer tours to Indonesia on Quicksilver's dime) but Johnson was beginning to chaff at the idea of living someplace he could drive nearly every square inch of in an hour. It was a nagging case of Island Fever that, following his older brothers' departures for college life at mainland colleges University of California, Los Angeles and University of Southern California, was particularly strong.

Johnson has tended to downplay the 'pro surfer' tag that has followed him throughout his life but became more prominent once his music career began to take off. 'It kind of gets exaggerated,' he said. 'I surfed in a few pro events when I was younger but I was never really a touring pro.'

Which is why he would often be amused when the stories about his alleged surfing prowess were conspicuous by their tendency to exaggerate. 'A lot of times I will read something and just crack up,' he explained to the *Oakland Tribune*. 'It was like I was going straight to the top of the surfing industry. I was just another kind of kid in Hawaii, who had a chance to do pro surfing on a light level.'

But even in his limited pro career, his raw skills immediately labeled him as a comer. Those who reported on the tournaments in Hawaii were quick to note his fearlessness in attacking a wave and his graceful approach to riding. He was rarely guilty of the kinds of style breaks that one tended to see in a less seasoned pro. He was definitely a crowd pleaser, especially when it came to the ladies who had become a large part of the surfing community.

Chris Mauro whose writing assignments for *Surfer* magazine gave him a ring side seat to many of Johnson's pro rides, related that Johnson had never placed higher than third in any tournament and was as good as the competition around him.

'Jack was good but he was like the equivalent of a golf pro at a golf course,' he said in a 2005 interview. 'He was as good as the others he competed against in Hawaii. But I don't think he could have been considered a world class pro at that point.'

Ever his worst critic, Johnson never saw himself as pro calibre.

'I was always good at good-sized surf in Oahu but I was never good at taking the time to milk the waves all the way to the beach,' he told the *Honolulu Weekly*. 'I didn't feel like I was ever going to be a contender on the world tour.'

Jack Johnson could have made a living as a pro. However by the time he turned 17, Johnson had made his decision. And long term his plans did not include surfing as a career. He knew on a spiritual level that surfing would always be a big part of his life. But he would not risk losing what it meant to him by doing what he loved for money.

He was literally caught in the middle. The reality was that he was good enough to at least give the pro circuit a try. But the reality was also that Johnson did not want to in anyway compromise the purity of the sport. In a sense he was selfish in that he wanted to keep it all to himself.

It was an attitude that was partially cultivated by a series of summer trips that Johnson took with his older brothers to Indonesia. It was the first time the youngster had been off the island and while he revelled in a surfing environment that was comparable to Oahu, more importantly he was among a different culture and people who lived their lives, to his way of thinking, in a quiet, peaceful and spiritual manner.

Johnson remained a good student throughout his high school years. He was still undecided about what he was going to do with his life but had proven particularly adept at mathematics and was thinking of that as a potential college major. He had applied to the University Of Southern California at Santa Barbara, the University Of California at San Diego and the University Of Hawaii.

For a while University Of Hawaii was Johnson's first choice because he was not sure he wanted to leave the islands. That stance softened and for a while then it was San Diego. But what it would finally boil down to was a passing comment by a family member who happened to mention that the surfing was good at Santa Barbara. Johnson was UCSB bound.

With his future seemingly in order, Johnson rode out his senior year secure in his choices and blissful in his devotion to conquering big waves. Shortly after he turned 17 in 1992, Johnson made history when he became the youngest surfer to compete in the prestigious Pipeline Masters, an annual Oahu tournament that drew the top surfers in the world to duel a Pipeline known for its perfect and often death-defying sets.

Johnson was at the top of his game at the Masters. He did not win the tournament but he had emerged as one of the stars of the future. The consensus was that it would only be a matter of time before he joined the elite group of globetrotting boardsmen.

One week after the tournament Johnson was once again back on North Shore; this time surfing the Pipeline for pleasure. He was riding a wave from the backside, which he would later admit was not his favourite way to ride. Johnson was nearing the end of a ride when he suddenly lost control of his board. A wave hit Johnson square in the back, knocking him off his board and face first into a dry coral reef bed and under the water.

'I was conscious under water but just barely,' he recalled of that frightful day. 'I wanted to keep resting down there. Getting to the surface was like a chore.'

Johnson lay momentarily dazed as the water swirled around his body. He was conscious enough to realise that he had to start swimming. He felt the onset of shock. He could not move.

'At that point I realised, "Okay, I'm going to drown here,"' he told *The Independent*.

When he regained his senses, the first thing he saw was blood. It was everywhere. He stood up and vomited. Johnson began running, unsteadily, down the beach toward his parent's home. Blood was pouring from several deep gashes on his face and head. His lip, nearly completely torn from his face, was flapping, spraying blood everywhere.

Jack Johnson thought he was going to die. Until he remembered that there was a paramedic living right next door to his house.

04

Jack Goes To College

Jeff and Patti Johnson had long ago gotten used to their kids getting banged up. Cuts and stitches were par for the course when your children surfed. But Trent remembered the phone call from his mother shortly after Johnson's crash.

'She said she wanted me to come see him but that I should not make any lame jokes,' he recalled in *Surfer* magazine. 'She said no matter what, just tell him he looks good.'

Johnson recalled the moment he appeared battered and bloody in front of his parents in a *Strand/China Business Weekly* interview: 'I walked into my front yard. My mom was there. She stayed pretty calm. My dad was making jokes and saying "Don't worry, chicks dig scars." My mom kept saying, "Oh Jeff, ssshhh!"'

The only known footage of the aftermath of Jack Johnson's horrific accident appears in a short interview clip that was part of a Quicksilver promotional surfing reel that would be released not long after Johnson's spill turned his face into hamburger. Years later Johnson would laughingly recall that he had not had much time to heal when the interview was shot and that he was not a pretty sight.

'I had no front teeth and this really big scar,' he said to *Rolling Stone*. 'There was also this big cut on my forehead and my lip was really fat because it had just been cut off. Even today, that's a pretty funny movie to watch.'

It was not funny the day Johnson's family and friends raced him to a nearby hospital's emergency room. The doctors gingerly cleaned away the blood to reveal a savage gash on his forehead, missing front teeth, a cracked skull, a piece of razor sharp coral sticking out of his skull and, most disturbing of all, his upper lip severed from nose to cheekbone. Doctors would work for hours to repair the damage. It would finally take more than 150 stitches to suture his wounds. A metal rod was permanently inserted in his upper jaw and two false teeth were put in place. Johnson would live. But he would carry the scars from this losing battle with the surf gods for the rest of his life.

'I got mug of the month in all the surf mags,' laughed Johnson in a *Q* magazine interview. 'And that upped my stock with the girls at school.'

On the surface, Johnson seemed to take the accident and his temporary disfigurement in his stride and appeared intent on getting on with his life. In Johnson's world view, the accident was all part of his karma; something to be dealt with and to simply move on. But he would later recall that his perception of mortality changed forever following the accident.

'I was feeling invincible at the time (of the accident),' he said in *Relix* magazine. 'For me, it was a serious wake-up call.'

But a wake-up call to what? At 17, the young man had only vague notions of what the future might bring. There were the hazy plans of going to college on the mainland which, upon deeper examination, might have seemed merely an excuse to spread his wings and experience the world. But when re-examining those early years, one clearly comes away feeling that the injury was just one more obstacle on a career path that, at that point, seemed unfocused.

Johnson left the hospital after several days of observation, joking with his loved ones that he now looked very much like the Frankenstein monster. He was prescribed bed rest and lots of it. Surfing would be out of the question for several months.

At first, Johnson was at a loss as to how to while away the hours he would normally have been surfing. But not too long after returning home, he picked up his guitar and started to play.

Johnson was not thinking of this unexpected side step from surfing to music as anything serious. In fact, he was still spending much of his days sitting on the sand, staring out at Pipeline and watching other people catch his waves. But the hobby slowly began to take over his thoughts.

Through sheer repetition, Johnson began to progress as a player. The sounds coming from the guitar seemed less halting and more fluid to his ears. His world view, in regards to music, was also broadening. Whereas before he was content to pick out the simple passages of Cat Stevens and Bob Marley, now he was beginning to explore artists with more complex musical agendas and deeper social messages.

One early example of his attempting to broaden his musical horizons came during an early amusing period in which Johnson fancied himself the reincarnation of Hendrix and attempted to duplicate those electric sounds on his battered acoustic. Johnson was less than enthusiastic about the sounds he made but, like everything else, he patiently kept at it and eventually found himself making musical sense of Hendrix's world and was able to run through some fairly decent acoustic-distortion passages.

In an old thrift shop not far from his home, he discovered an old Woody Guthrie album. He also began to listen to Bob Dylan with more than a passing interest. Lyrics and the stories they told had always been of keen interest to Johnson and, in Guthrie and Dylan, he was finding a sense of language as power and more than a bit of inspiration.

It was not long into his convalescence that Johnson began concentrating on writing his own songs. Unlike his compositions for Limber Chicken, those first efforts were wistful, sing-a-long odes, much in keeping with the mood and vibe of the informal party sets he encountered growing up and thinly disguised homages to his musical heroes.

Johnson has often winced at the mention of those early efforts, tending to dismiss them as not very good. Despite having sung at the aforementioned beach parties, his writing talents were not the only thing the self-doubting Johnson was feeling. Johnson was still not confident in his vocals, even in the privacy of his own room. But he was slowly coming around to the idea that his singing voice, which has been described on several occasions as a wispy drawl, was not really so bad.

During his recuperation there was concern among Johnson's family and friends that the severity of the accident and his injuries had resulted in a psychological barrier that would keep him out of the water. But, if anything, the accident had only fuelled his passion for the surf and, in his Zen terms, the battle between man and nature. And so, a bit more than two months after slamming face first into the coral reef bed, John-

son was paddling his board back out on the Pipeline as if nothing had
happened.

The youngster had grown up on a steady and willing diet of surfing documentaries but the idea of actually being in one had never really crossed
his mind. Until word came down in 1993 that famed *Endless Summer*
filmmaker Bruce Brown would be coming to Oahu to film surfers on the
Pipeline for his follow up to that classic, *Endless Summer 2*. Word had
gotten to Brown of the youthful Johnson's prowess and so he was selected
to be one of many locals whose exploits would be immortalised in the
film that would be released in 1994. Those privy to the filming have often
related that Johnson was taking the *Endless Summer 2* experience fairly
seriously and had been eager to show off his fancy surfing moves.

Johnson finished his senior year of high school with solid, if not spectacular grades, a diploma in hand. His return to surfing served as therapy
of sorts; a way to escape thoughts of an immediate future that was nothing if not scattered. The idea of a career in pro surfing was still tugging at
him. Coming to grips with an academic life and higher education made
sense logically but emotionally it was leaving him a bit cold.

The alternative, most likely, would be a blue-collar, dead-end service
job within the tourist industry; complete with a steady pay cheque but
not much of a future or to follow his father into the construction trade.
Ultimately Johnson decided, in the best Hawaiian tradition, to just roll
with whatever came his way.

He was pleasantly surprised when he was finally accepted by the University Of Southern California at Santa Barbara for the fall 1993 semester. Rather than be happy that his future, at least for the short term, had
been decided, Johnson remained in turmoil. He felt that he would be
able to balance the normal life at college with his passion for surfing and
the spiritual elements that entailed. But as he counted down the days to
leaving for California and higher education, Johnson was having second
thoughts about his decision.

'You grow up here and, as a kid, all you know is your island,' he said
in a *Los Angeles Times* interview. 'Then you start thinking about going
somewhere else and all of a sudden you're thinking, "Oh my god, this
world is gigantic."'

He was also troubled by the fact that many of his lifelong friends from
the island had, in fact, plunged into the world of professional surfing;

had begun to make serious money and were touring the world as the new wave of superstar surfers. And Johnson had to admit that he was a bit jealous.

'When I left for college, I watched my friends surf professionally,' he told *Sports Illustrated*. 'They were travelling all over the world and it was tough. I thought I'd made a mistake choosing such a normal life.'

But the even-handed nature of Johnson's thought process eventually brought him around to another way of thinking about the pro surf life he was leaving behind.

'Surfing is a little bubble of its own,' he told the *Strand/China Business Week*. 'But then you step outside that bubble and you look back, and it's just a little microcosm. It's very macho and there's a lot of ego involved in the surfing world. It's nice for me to get out of it a little bit.'

The young man's final decision was not made any easier by the fact that his father was not necessarily in his corner when it came to leaving Oahu for the mainland and higher education. Johnson remembered his father's parting words on the day he packed his bags.

'The day I left for college he was trying to talk me out of it,' recalled Johnson in a *Rolling Stone* interview. 'He said, "There are a lot of people over there (on the mainland) and it's really easy to just feel like a number." He almost had me convinced.'

In the end, Johnson sided with normalcy and left Hawaii for the shores of sunny Southern California. What he found was somewhat familiar. The beaches along the Santa Barbara coastline, with prime surfing spots like Miramar Beach, were comforting to the transplanted islander. Santa Barbara, a mixture of big city and suburban sprawl that stopped right at the edge of the Pacific Ocean, was fuelled by a largely under-25 student population, reflecting a hang-loose lifestyle and attitude very much in keeping with his island upbringing. But as he settled into his dorm room at Anacapa Hall and ate his first meal at the DLG dining common, Johnson was feeling very much alone.

And alone for Johnson came with a capital A. In his isolation he would describe the experience as like being an alien from another planet.

Culturally, Johnson also was finding himself behind the curve. Santa Barbara drew students from major urban cities whose attitudes and knowledge Johnson found sophisticated in comparison to the simple, laidback values and world view he had grown up around. And he laughingly recalled how he would often play at humour to avoid being considered dumb.

'You know when somebody talks about something and you don't really know what it is they're talking about but you feel embarrassed because you feel like you should already know?' said Johnson. 'I'd just say, "Oh I'm sorry. I'm from Hawaii."'

Johnson's feelings of being alone were tempered, somewhat, during his first week on campus by a chance meeting in the campus dining area with a pretty blonde education major named Kim. It was a meeting that he would chronicle in the song 'Bubble Toes.' Their initial meeting was a literal stare-down contest. Johnson stared at the young woman as she was looking for a place to sit. She caught his stare but would not look away. This went on for about 20 seconds before both of them started laughing. Kim walked over to Johnson and sat down at his table.

Johnson would recall in later years that he had been completely blindsided by Kim. 'I went to college looking to play the field a little bit,' he laughingly recalled to *The Independent*. 'Then one week in, I met Kim.'

As he would quickly discover, Kim was very much like himself; bright, spiritual and straightforward in her dealings with people and somebody who embraced the world around her in every possible way.

Kim recalled in a *Honolulu Weekly* feature that she had grown up in a family of teachers. 'Everyone taught. Uncles, grandparents, parents, everyone. I always knew that one day, I would too. Teachers tend to believe in doing the right thing, taking care of people and communities. I think the sense of living right and doing good in the world was passed onto me.'

Johnson was quietly outgoing and shy around her, which had always been his way around the opposite sex. It was a side of his nature that Kim found instantly appealing. The couple did not officially date for about a month; preferring to feel each other out in the context of a group that included a group of mutual friends. Finally one night she kissed him. It might not have been love at first sight but it was the beginning of a slow, steady relationship that would continue to deepen in the weeks and months that followed.

'I was eighteen and I had a lot of confidence, but I'd never met a girl like this before,' he confessed in a *Strand/China Business Week* interview. 'She was beautiful and charming and seemed so out of my league. She was so much smarter than me. She was only eighteen and she'd already read the beat poets and she knew about Jack Kerouac and Allen Ginsberg.'

Years later Johnson would acknowledge that he had been so instantly attracted to Kim that the relationship would, indirectly, impact his first year academic difficulties. He felt that Kim was so much smarter than him and so, in an attempt to impress her, he ended up enrolling in several very difficult classes that he was really not interested in. That this was Johnson's response to a strong woman indicated a high degree of insecurity for this stranger in a literal strange land.

Kim would be the first of many friends Johnson would make during his first semester at UCSB. Johnson tended to bond with people much like himself, surfers or creative types and in particular musicians. One of those would be a fellow free spirit named Zach Gill, the leader of a local jam band called Django (which would later become Animal Liberation Orchestra), who was the living embodiment of the easy going Santa Barbara lifestyle. Like Johnson, Gill was a fairly laidback personality, prone to enthusiastic outbursts and equally contemplative moods. After Kim, Gill was the person Johnson would be closest to during his college years.

Once settled personally and academically, Johnson's life became fairly routine. He would go to class, surf and with Kim go to the movies or hang out at local clubs. It was during the latter outings that Johnson experienced an even more diverse musical world. Alternative rock and jazz were very much on the Santa Barbara menu, as were the occasional last gasps of punk. Sometimes there would be a folk singer on stage and Johnson would inwardly marvel at the simplicity of one man and one guitar.

Through Gill, Johnson was introduced to the Santa Barbara music scene on a fairly informal level with Gill and Johnson getting together occasionally in the dorms and jamming informally. For Johnson, who still remained self-conscious on the musical front, it was baby steps.

During that first year, Johnson would regularly call home and he would often joke with his father, Jeff, that he would wind up being a rich statistician when he graduated from college. But hidden behind the jokes was the sad reality that being a math major had quickly gone from a good idea to a dry, emotionless exercise. In his private moments, Johnson would often revisit those last comments his father had made to him before he left Oahu. And in a literal sense, he now found them prophetic.

Johnson would daydream through classes, struggling to show the slightest interest in numbers. His thoughts would inevitably turn to Kelly Slater and his friends from the island; friends who had entered the professional surfing world and were regularly riding the waves in remote outposts of the world. His heart was not in it and it showed in early grades that were less than stellar.

'I was a math major and I felt like a failure,' he said in *Launch* magazine. 'I remember during the first quarter at UCSB, I was sure I would go home. I was like, "I'm going to go back home and surf. This is getting old."'

Midway through his freshman year and Johnson was already at a crossroads. It would not have taken much for him to abandon the notion of an academic life. It was not too late for him to give the professional surfing circuit a real shot. And truth be known, Johnson missed his family much more than he thought he would.

Whenever there was a break in the school year, Johnson would pack his bags, leave campus, return to his home in Oahu and surf the Pipeline for a day or two. His parents were understanding of his predicament and would listen to his feelings about how unhappy he was. But wisely they left any future decisions up to him. And Johnson's decision was always to return to UCSB. The reason being that Kim was there and Johnson was, by this time, deeply in love.

With Kim's help and encouragement, Johnson finally settled into some semblance of a routine. He continued to attend classes. He was trying his best to get into the complex world of numbers but was still not happy. But he was determined to stick it out until he found something he really wanted to do.

Surfing continued to be a therapeutic diversion from the grind of academic life. He would be on the water as often as possible and would find a whole new set of friends along the way. He became tight with a musician-surfer named Ted Lennon after a chance meeting at an art gallery. But the seeds for a different kind of life were planted the day he met brothers and cousins Chris, Emmett and Brendan Malloy.

The Malloys were instinctive entrepreneurs who had managed to turn their love of surfing and filmmaking into a profitable business making surf documentaries and rock music videos. Their goal of combining business with pleasure was significant in the eyes of the impressionable Johnson. They never let business get in the way of having a good time or a good ride.

Johnson was instantly taken by the sincerity of the Malloys. They were honest in an earthy, no nonsense way. And when he inevitably got around to looking at their documentaries, he was impressed with what he saw. Yes, there was much in their films that catered to the prevailing, somewhat low brow attitude of surf films. But there was a subtle sense of majesty that was also apparent. Johnson saw them as artists, creative spirits very much in synch with his own attitudes toward the nature of things.

Through the Malloys' experiences and stories, Johnson began to see the possibilities of a life on the waves that he had never before considered. Although the purist in him continued to be leery of combining his love for the water with a money making venture.

Johnson was continuing to find that Santa Barbara had quite a music scene going on. In small clubs and at spontaneous beach parties in and around the city, he would continue to absorb everything from hardcore punk to the latest experimental-alternative bands to classic rock and examples of the jam band explosion that had grown out of the Phish and Grateful Dead experience. He became particularly enamoured of the burgeoning jam band genre and often marvelled at how bands like Phish could cram so much creativity into music that often seemed to go on forever. Johnson was amazed and inspired and now aspiring to do the same thing.

He found himself turning more and more to his music and in a more serious manner. Practicing all hours of the day and night, Johnson was slowly but surely forging a sound, mellow but lyrically challenging and quite simple in execution. Johnson would often recall that those days were marked by frustration that would often manifest itself in his song-writing.

'I remember there were days that I was supposed to be writing papers for school. I didn't want to but I had to,' he recalled in a 91X radio interview. 'But I would find myself sitting around, writing songs instead.'

Johnson returned to Oahu at Christmas to visit his family. It was the first time he brought Kim with him and he was thrilled when his family and friends welcomed her like a member of the family. Johnson used the holidays as an opportunity to reconnect with Kelly Slater and other old time surfing buddies. He took in their stories of life on the pro circuit and expressed no small amount of jealousy. He passed his days surfing the Pipeline and the nights in the Johnsons' front yard, eating, drinking and, yes, singing with his friends. Jack Johnson was at peace for the first time in a long time.

Shortly after their return to Santa Barbara, fate and the love of his life stepped in to steer Johnson to his true passion.

One night Kim took Johnson to the UCSB Film Department's Reel Loud Film Festival, a collection of short films created by students. Johnson sat in the auditorium, his eyes wide and his mouth open, as he was bombarded with creative, truly amazing images accompanied by equally expressive soundtracks. By the time he left the screening that night, Johnson had decided to drop maths and become a film major.

'When I switched to a film major, I learned what it was like to put time into something you really want to spend your time doing,' he told a *Chicago Innerview* reporter. 'Suddenly I was getting A's in all my classes and I didn't even feel like I was working. For me, film was about finding the thing in your life that lights a spark and you feel like you are, naturally, very good at it.'

Plunging into this strange and wonderful new world did not change Johnson that much. He remained humble and instinctively capable to those who knew him. According to UCSB film studies lecturer Dana Driskel, he was that rarity, a filmmaker without an ego.

'Between surfing and trying to do cinematography anywhere and anytime he could, he had a passion for music and was fully involved in almost everything,' said Driskel in a *Daily Nexus* feature. 'He was always supportive of the other filmmakers. He might have been aware that he was talented but he never made a big thing of it.'

Johnson's immersion in film resulted in a more upbeat attitude toward the education process. In film he was constantly being overwhelmed with free flowing ideas. He was surprised at the seemingly constant state of inspiration he found himself in. And he was in good company. Those majoring in film at UCSBs were, inevitably, free thinkers who ran the emotional gamut from very serious to very crazy. Students saw a lot of films, tinkered with ageing camera equipment and made their own little movies in a climate that encouraged creative exploration. Education was fun and Johnson was happy.

Johnson immersed himself into every aspect of the filmmaking process. He took classes in production, film history and film theory. A course in Japanese cinema taught him the wonders of Kurosawa and Ozu. A similar class in French film taught him a fondness for Goddard and Truffaut.

Johnson proved a natural in this new milleu. He had a keen eye for style and a real sense of how to use the camera to capture the perfect moment; something endless hours of watching surfers and surf movies had instilled in him. He worked really hard within the context of a film programme that was predictably fly by the seat of your pants.

'I worked really hard making films,' he remembered in a *Launch* magazine article. 'It was a lot of late nights, staying up, working on these black and white independent films and then trying not to fall asleep in class the next day. We'd trade off. I'd act in these dumb films for friends and then they'd act for me because nobody else would want to be in our films because we didn't know how to use the equipment. We were making really bad films for years. But it was fun and eventually I learned how to use the equipment which made it even better.'

Johnson moved out of Anacapa Hall at the conclusion of his first year at UCSB and into a small apartment in the nearby college town of Isla Vista. Literally the equivalent of New York's Greenwich Village, Isla Vista was a small seaside community bound together by a handful of convenience stores, a couple of watering holes and a whole lot of college students heavily into the arts and music.

'I was definitely in good company in Isla Vista,' recalled Johnson in a *Daily Nexus* feature. 'The cool thing I loved about that town was that everyone had drums, basses, amps and guitars set up in their garages. I would be riding down the street to a friend's house and I would see and hear music everywhere.'

With all the creative energy in the air, it was natural that it would end up influencing Johnson's maturing approach to songwriting. A sponge when it came to soaking up images and impressions, he would often end up turning those visions into lyrics. 'It was just kind of what was going on in my head at the time. For me, the visual and the sound just kind of went together.'

Johnson's songwriting was becoming tighter, more assured and somewhat less sing-a-long in nature. However the progress could still only be measured in baby steps. The songs were continuing in the wispy, mellow vein; simple chord progressions painting pretty lyrical pictures of a laid-back life. But Johnson had also begun to discover influences in bands and singer-songwriters who were using folk stylings as a jumping-off point for a more detailed, divergent and progressive sound.

The sturdy instrumentation and stridently old-school vocals of G. Love & Special Sauce were a particular favourite of Johnson's at the time. But it would be during the many late nights of not enough sleep and just enough beer that the music of Ben Harper, a veteran performer who was combining folk and rock elements into an often-message-driven music, that would begin to shape his musical world.

'I heard Ben Harper's record *Fight For Your Mind* in college and it truly inspired me,' he said in *Interview* magazine. 'Ben's music had all that rebellion and aggression, but in a pure way. Until then, I hadn't found what I wanted to do with music. He made me realise that you don't have to have distortion on your guitar to make music that mattered.'

Now more confident, Johnson was much more open when it came to showing off what he still perceived to be only so-so musical skills. Zach Gill, The Malloys, Ted Lennon and others in his growing circle of surfer-musician friends were immediately impressed with his compositions and a decent, if not spectacular, singing voice.

Much of the credit for Johnson's musical coming out most certainly lay in the constant encouragement of Kim. As their relationship deepened, she became the initial sounding board for any new song. She found that encouraging her lover was not always easy. Johnson was his own worst enemy when it came to assessing his talents. He felt his voice was weak and that he did not project well. And even with the injection of G. Love and Ben Harper into his life, he still felt that the majority of his songs were fairly lightweight and forgettable. But Kim persisted in selling him on the idea that his voice was fine and that his songs were very good. Eventually he began to believe her.

Johnson continued to climb out of his shell; graduating from performing at beach parties and Isla Vista keggers to the occasional small club set which, despite the expected nerves, he handled with a ragged kind of polish. Sometimes he would be backed by Gill, other members of the Animal Liberation Orchestra, or whoever happened to be available. But more often than not, it was simply Johnson alone with his guitar.

Johnson's comfort level with live performing finally reached a point where he formed a legitimate rock and roll band. Soil, a band Johnson put together with some UCSB classmates with an eye toward playing some parties and making a few bucks, was a big step up from his Limber Chicken days. Soil played a mixture of good time rock cover tunes and a smattering of originals, all of which were penned by Johnson. For Johnson, it was the next tentative step into the public eye.

Soil's reputation as a good time party band spread quickly among the student and surfing population in and around Santa Barbara, Isla Vista and nearby Ventura. The band was good and, of equal importance, available at the drop of a hat for a reasonable amount of money or a keg of beer. They were not getting rich but they were having a hell of a time.

'We were fairly decent,' said Johnson to radio station 91X. 'We were a fun party band. We actually opened for Dave Matthews once right before he became really famous. It was at the Ventura Theatre and I remember that the place was only about a third full. We also opened for Sublime just when they were starting to get big. The Sublime show was kind of a funny gig. It was rumoured that Sublime were not going to show up and we ended up playing about a half hour more than we were supposed to because the club owner kept telling us "They're not here yet, keep playing." So yeah, it was a fun band and we had a lot of good times.'

Soil was the first time Johnson put his original songs out in front of large crowds. Content to play guitar while another member of the band sang, Johnson would, nevertheless, find himself beaming with pride when one of his original compositions received thunderous applause from an audience.

Johnson was quietly confident in his emerging talents and the fact that he was finally willing to put his songs out there for public scrutiny. But that confident streak stopped when it was time for somebody to step up to the mike and sing them. At that moment Johnson would sink into the background and let somebody else sing them. Because at that moment he did not think he could sing a lick.

Eventually Johnson decided that one of his favourite songs, 'Flake', was something he just had to sing and so, toward the end of Soil's run, he began to close the band's set by singing in a big live setting for the first time. Those who witnessed it offered that while not always pitch perfect, Johnson's vocals were fairly good.

Soil's main competition on the Santa Barbara-Isla Vista party circuit were Django and Johnson's good friend Gill. There was a good natured rivalry between the two bands and the two friends who often ended up playing the same venue on the same night. But Johnson recalls that the rivalry never got too serious.

'I started thinking of our rivalry as being like the cartoon show Jem and the Misfits,' Johnson told *Pop, Rock and Jazz*. 'It boiled down to whoever bought the most kegs of beer won. And most of the time things were pretty darn equal.'

ALO bass player Steve Adams remembered those days in a conversation with *Music In Schools Today*. 'We each had our own bands but we'd go see each other play and sometimes we'd get to do shows together. We'd always get together when the bands weren't playing and just play for fun at our houses. We'd make things up on the spot or teach each other songs.'

Adams recalled that toward the end of their respective college careers, when Django had morphed into Animal Liberation Orchestra, that Johnson began spending even more time in their musical world. 'Toward the end of college, when ALO was starting to play out more regularly, Jack would often come and sit in with the band. We'd learn a few of his songs and be his backing band somewhere in the middle of an ALO set.'

Soil eventually went the way of all party bands and broke up. But by that time, Johnson and the guys in Animal Liberation Orchestra had become extremely tight and would often spend hours on end in their small Isla Vista apartments, jamming well into the wee hours.

Johnson's creative energies would be spread all over the map during his college years. His music and songwriting skills had grown into a kind of urban legend in and around the Santa Barbara area; with more than one person suggesting that Johnson seek a recording contract. But he gently rebuffed those suggestions. Music, like surfing, had become pure to him and he intended on keeping it that way.

Four years of intensive film studies had turned Johnson into a competent cameraman with a solid sense of framing and visual style. Although offering nothing definite, the Malloy brothers hinted that they might have some work for him once he graduated. His true passion remained surfing and he indulged in it at every opportunity.

The Malloys remained Johnson's unspoken mentors and, when they felt his filmmaking chops were up to the task, they offered him his first professional gigs. Johnson held the camera on the Taylor Steele-Chris Malloy surf film *All For One*. He handled the camera during the comedy elements of Steele's next movie *The Show*. Now engrained in the Malloy filmmaking machine, he was also on the crews that did the music videos for the bands Unwritten Law, Blink-182 and The Foo Fighters. Johnson's ability with the camera soon landed him a couple of jobs shooting commercials as well as a freelance gig for a local stock photo agency which had him shooting pictures of people walking up and down the beach.

Johnson's relationship with Kim had endured the stresses and challenges of college life as well as his status as a local pop star. She had always been comfortable with his surfing, supportive of his film studies and, perhaps most importantly, was never jealous of the attention shown him by other women when he performed. In return, Johnson remained completely faithful to Kim. Theirs was the perfect melding of spiritual and emotional compatibility, things the pressures of a material world could never intrude on.

A big plus in their relationship was a clear sense of where it seemed to be going. They sensed that their feelings for each other would ultimately end in marriage. And it bode well for the long term that Kim was realistic about the chances of them leading anything but a normal lifestyle.

'We always thought that I would have the steady job and that he would have his freelance work,' she recalled in a *Sports Illustrated* feature. 'I could never expect him to conform to normal work hours.'

Jack Johnson graduated from the University Of Southern California at Santa Barbara with a 3.0 grade point average and a BA degree in film in 1997. Now all he had to do was figure out what to do with it.

05

Around The World In 80 Waves

Johnson and Kim celebrated their respective graduations in 1997 by getting away from it all.

The couple jetted to Europe where they spent the summer leisurely travelling across the continent in a VW van. Seeing parts of the world for the first time was an eye-opening experience for the couple. They were humbled in a spiritual sense by the ghosts of ancient civilizations that spoke to them in the ruins, in the cobble-stone and dirt streets and in the centuries old buildings.

Johnson was particularly struck by the simplicity and the peaceful-ness as they passed through villages and towns and observed different nationalities and cultures spending their lives much as their ancestors had before them. The couple often came upon majestic ocean vistas where Johnson would take the opportunity to test the surf on foreign shores.

The van, nicknamed the UMP because of the letters UMP on the license plates, was very much dictating the course their vacation took. When it broke down, which was quite often, that was where the couple stayed until the van could be repaired. After several transportation starts and stops, their trip came to a rather unceremonious end in Florence, Italy when the van suddenly veered out of control and crashed into the side of a building.

When Johnson called home to sadly recount their latest automotive misadventure, he was informed by his parents that Chris Malloy had called and that he was looking for him. Johnson loved a mystery and Kim and he had seen just about everything Europe had to offer them at the time and so they said goodbye to UMP and booked a flight back to the states.

Much like his father's solo voyage to Hawaii, the long flight back to the states gave Johnson a chance to think about the future and how he was going to make a living. His skills with a camera made him more than qualified for any number of jobs. But he knew in his head and heart that whatever he did, he did not want to be too far from the surf. He sensed that any offer coming from the Malloys would almost certainly put him exactly where he wanted to be. Which was on the water, shooting film and documenting the sport he loved.

Admittedly, Johnson had arrived with a different mindset when it came to the technical aspects of shooting a surf video that was part and parcel of what he had seen and experienced growing up. 'There was this era that I kind of grew up in,' he told *Los Angeles City Beat*. 'Jack McCoy's films were probably the most popular when I was growing up. Then Taylor Steele came along and his were all shot on video to real fast punk rock music. As a kid, you were just into seeing the tricks and listening to the music. But once I went to school and started working with 16mm, I don't think I would have ever made a surf movie if it was just on video.'

Given his connection and work history with the Malloys, as well as his own affinity for surfing and filmmaking, it almost seemed a natural that Johnson would inevitably follow the likes of Bruce Brown and Taylor Steele and jump right into making his own surf films. But he was hesitant and, much like with his music, for a simple reason.

Quite simply, Johnson was not sure he would be, emotionally, up to the task of watching his friends surf some of the biggest waves in the world while he would be limited to just shooting the fun with a camera.

While he was hesitant to take that professional step, Johnson had long ago laid out a mental blueprint of what a Jack Johnson surf movie would be. What the budding filmmaker envisioned was a radical departure from the sensationalist, low brow humour that populated the spaces in between the inevitable big wave shots of most films. Johnson was always big on feeling and saw his ideal surf movie as conveying, through powerful images and music, something special and personal.

'For me, surfing was kind of a whole way of life, the culture and the family of it,' he explained in a *Surfing Vancouver Island* story. 'That's what I would try to get across in the films.'

As the reality of having to make a living set in, Johnson eventually decided that surf filmmaking might be the way to point his career if, in fact, he could make the films his way.

In typical Jack Johnson fashion, he eventually saw the simple logic in the decision: he knew how to work a camera and had grown up with all the people who had gone on to become big time surfers and so, obviously he had the connections.

'The best thing was that I could film when the light was good and I could surf when the light wasn't good,' he told *Hooked On The Outdoors*.

The more he thought about it, the more Johnson seemed to gravitate toward this way of prolonging his self-proclaimed bohemian lifestyle a bit longer and to be responsible.

'We'd get just enough money to pay the bills and I'd have a reason to travel to all these great spots,' he told *Strand/China Business Week*. 'At that point, I thought that making surf movies would be my career.'

These were the thoughts going through Johnson's head when the flight from Italy touched down in the states and the couple returned to Santa Barbara where they set up residence in a small apartment. While he still had Oahu in his heart, and would often return for visits, Johnson had found Santa Barbara and nearby Isla Vista the perfect substitute. The surfing, in particular Miramar Beach and the close proximity to Malibu, was comparable in most respects to Pipeline and he had grown fond of the people. Most relevant in Johnson's life plan, however, was the fact that Kim could pursue her master's degree in education while teaching high school maths to pay the bills.

Not long after returning home, Johnson contacted Chris Malloy who laid out his plans for what would ultimately become the surfing documentary *Thicker Than Water*.

Thicker Than Water, as envisioned by Malloy, seemed the ideal first film for Johnson. It would be produced by the Malloy brothers which would offer the rookie filmmaker a certain degree of comfort. The film would be shot entirely in 16 millimeter, a technique that four years of college had made Johnson quite proficient at.

Thicker Than Water would feature professional surfers Kelly Slater, Rob

Machado, Timmy Curren, Benji Weatherley, Shane Dorian, Brad Gerlach, Babby Martinez, Conan Hayes, Noah Johnson, Saxon Boucher and
Taylor Knox. The literal who's who of the professional surfing circuit was
also a laundry list of familiar faces and long-time friends that Johnson
had grown up with and who he respected as athletes and people.

In the ideal surf filmmaking world, the filmmaker was also the surfer's
buddy; somebody they could trust to be responsible when filming and,
equally important, somebody they knew they could joke around with
and share a beer when the camera was not in use.

The concept was also something that appealed to Johnson's filmmaking
aesthetic. Rather than the typical big waves and lame humour highjinx,
Thicker Than Water's ambitious tour of locales in Indonesia, Tahiti, India,
Ireland, France, Hawaii and New York City would have a more spiritual
tone; going beyond the notion of the ocean as playground to focus on the
surfers and the people they met as fellow travellers in a world steeped in
nature and a natural order of things.

This was not going to be an easy shoot. The around-the-world odyssey
would take 18 months with only sporadic breaks. It went without saying
that Kim and Johnson would miss each other immensely. But they both
understood that it was something that Johnson had to do.

It was like a grand reunion when Johnson met up with the movie's
surfers. He had not seen some of these people in years and so there was
a lot of catching up to do. Johnson knew that this was going to be an
easy ride, just a bunch of good friends filming one large postcard of their
endless day at the beach.

The weeks and months spent shooting *Thicker Than Water* (produced
by Chris and Emmett Malloy) were the embodiment of high adventure
for Johnson. The route the filmmakers took had only been partially
planned out, which left a lot of room for surprises.

While in India, they heard stories of a place far off the beaten track
where the waves were legendary and, without giving it a second thought,
hired a boat to take them there. The detour resulted in some majestic
footage of surf riding in the Bay Of Bengal. The familiar surf spots of
Indonesia took on a heightened perspective with Johnson and his bulky
Bolex camera at hand. Johnson's humanity would regularly make its way
into the footage he was filming.

'A lot of the time we were in uncharted territories,' he recalled of the

trip in a *Detours* interview. 'At one point, we were looking for these islands off the coast of India. We found a fisherman who took us down to
a bay and then we jumped onto a boat that took us out in the middle of
the ocean and we spent weeks surfing and fishing for food.'

Scenes of the people they met in their travels and their interaction with
these globetrotting surfers were captured in a loving-candid manner that
made the most of natural light and masterful close ups. Johnson was also
proving more than capable of adding a new dimension to the de facto
surfing footage. Whether shot from the boat or, sometimes, in the water,
the surf proved a natural pallet in which Johnson excelled in the use of
odd angles, prolonged, all-encompassing long shots and the often surreal
use of refracted light and shadow to add substance and depth to even the
most casual ride.

Johnson was proving a subtle filmmaker on the *Thicker Than Water*
shoot. He was all but invisible to the subjects of the film, capturing quiet
and all-too-human moments as well as the emotions of exhilaration and
joy and painting them quite naturally into the context of their exotic
surroundings.

When filming, Johnson was intent and intense. He immersed himself
in the process and his equipment. But, as predicted, when the sun went
down or some unexpected cloud banks cut the light, he was quick to grab
up his surfboard and join his friends on the mountainous waves.

Make no mistake, the journey that became *Thicker Than Water* was not
an easy one. Johnson's body was sunburned raw and peeling from the
constant exposure to the sun. The exposure to surf wax on a daily basis
aided the sun in the peeling process and, when coupled with the weeks
old growth of beard, gave Johnson and his crew the look of shipwrecked
sailors. Johnson would admit that he was always tired and usually had
just enough strength to crawl into his rack and go to sleep.

Always lurking on the edge of his surfing adventures was Johnson's
music. Inevitably after a long day of filming and surfing, the group would
get together for a seafood dinner around a campfire or on the gently bobbing deck of a boat in the middle of the South Pacific, drink some of the
local brew and swap stories and rehash the adventures of the day. And it
was an equal certainty that, at some point, somebody would suggest that
Johnson take out his guitar and play a few songs.

Which he did.

For many of those on the trip, this was the first time they had prolonged exposure to Johnson and his music. In particular, the Malloys were shocked by what they perceived as the quiet power in Johnson's lyrics and voice.

For Johnson, the constant exposure to the majesty of the ocean, the spirituality of the people they met and the places they visited were a jolt to his creativity. In a ragged notebook, he began to fill pages with lines and snatches of lyrics.

'I kind of switch frames of mind,' Johnson once explained of his songwriting process during his filmmaking days in *Launch* magazine. 'Going to a new place a lot of times gives me ideas for new songs.'

And although the documentation remains scattered and inconsistent, the consensus was that several of the songs that would become Jack Johnson standards in later years were conceived in whole or part during the long days and nights filming *Thicker Than Water*. Surfer Rob Machado has claimed, somewhat tongue-in-cheek, that an early version of the song 'Flake' was written in a seaside hotel room during that trip. For his part, Johnson has recalled that the song 'Rodeo Clowns' came into being as the result of people-watching in nightclubs in three different countries on that trip.

'Before the trip started, I had written a verse and then put the song away. In Australia I wrote the first verse,' he related in a 91X radio interview. ' When we were down in Tahiti I wrote another one. I think I wrote the last verse in Ireland. It's all the same song. It was just us sitting in three different nightclubs in three different parts of the world and watching people.'

Johnson felt a strong affinity for the idea of encroaching technology which resulted in his writing the song 'Holes To Heaven' which also saw life during the *Thicker Than Water* odyssey.

Like many of Johnson's songs, 'Holes To Heaven' had a simple, philosophical origin. During the trip, their boat kept breaking down and they had to keep going back to port for repairs. Johnson put that simple notion and his own take on how technology, in this very small way, was conspiring to keep the surfers from reaching the surf. Thus 'Holes To Heaven' was born.

It was during the weeks and months of the seemingly endless voyage that Johnson, at the encouragement of surfer friends Slater and Machado, began making primitive four-track recordings of his songs. Johnson saw nothing out of the ordinary in his musical efforts and did not think twice about handing out copies of his music to anybody who asked.

Johnson was in regular contact with Kim throughout the *Thicker Than Water* shoot. He was happy to see that she was keeping herself busy. She was constantly encouraging Johnson's efforts and never complained about being the primary breadwinner in a relationship separated by many thousands of miles. If anything, being apart only seemed to strengthen the bonds between them. The love Johnson felt for Kim had deepened with the knowledge that she was selflessly doing everything she could to help make his dreams and ambitions a reality.

'Kim supported me as I travelled around the world making surfing films,' he said in an *Outside* magazine interview. 'And that was on a teacher's salary.'

The *Thicker Than Water* journey ended in 1998 with Johnson and the Malloys returning to Santa Barbara and almost immediately entering into the editing process of the film. Looking at the footage from the shoot for the first time under ideal conditions was a revelation to the true talents of Johnson as a filmmaker.

There was a true sense of rapture and raw power to the big wave sequences and a truly spiritual sense of balance between the pure drive of the surfers in their pursuit of the perfect wave and their relationship to the world around them. Much more than a series of monster wave shots, *Thicker Than Water* pushed humanity to the forefront of each and every image.

The editing session was a largely informal affair with the filmmaker's friends dropping by at all hours to watch the film slowly come together under Johnson's instinctive touch. Among those paying a visit was Johnson's surf buddy J.P. Plunier, a much respected music producer whose credits included Johnson's idol Ben Harper.

Johnson often recalled that Plunier would pop in anytime of the day or night and look over Johnson's shoulder as he was editing the film and sit transfixed at the majesty of Johnson's raw footage.

Inevitably talk began among the filmmakers about an accompanying soundtrack to the film. Bands as diverse as G. Love & Special Sauce and The Chieftians were being considered. But of a more immediate concern was the adding of background music to the surfing and interview sequences. Johnson seemed the logical choice for the job. It seemed like a fairly easy task; laying down easy going acoustic instrumental passages and the occasional shred of vocal to set the scene for what was going to be in the film.

'When it was time to edit the film, we had this little four-track player set up next to the editing machine,' Johnson related in *Xpress Online*. 'The whole idea was that I was going to make these rough little sketches on the four-track and then go into the studio. But we just ended up getting attached to those four-track recordings and so we put those in the movie. It was useful because you could put lyrics where you wanted or you could leave them out where you wanted.'

By this time, Johnson had become fairly comfortable singing and play-ing in front of his friends. Playing softly in the quiet and the dim light of the editing bay into a four-track recorder was, by association, a liberating experience; his crisp, bluesy licks and soft, soulful vocals working in time with the images on the editing bay screen. Composing the original music for *Thicker Than Water* got Johnson to thinking about what he might be able to do with his music now that it was suddenly becoming more than a hobby.

But the singer's insecurities about taking a higher profile continued to blunt his ambitions. He was secure in the knowledge that he could write songs, that he could sing them comfortably with a small circle of friends and that he could actually record them alone in a darkened room. But he felt he was far from ready to play live and he really did not believe there was an album's worth of substantive music in him.

The first screening of the completed cut of *Thicker Than Water* was a resounding success. Although the Malloys were instrumental in guiding the direction and tone of the movie, the just-under-an-hour documentary was very much Jack Johnson's baby. His cinematic tone, the dance with light and shadow and the glorious large and intimate moments immedi-ately struck the audience as an insightful new wave of surf documentary filmmaking. The raves were equally great for Johnson's musical backings that flickered seamlessly in and out of the panorama.

Thicker Than Water was released in 1999 and the film and Johnson be-came the new gods of the surfing community. Unbeknownst to Johnson, his music, much in the tradition of Grateful Dead tape traders, had gone to bootleg heaven. His surfing buddies who had received the original four-track tapes from Johnson, had been secretly burning copies onto CDs and passing them along to friends who, in turn, did the same. With the release of *Thicker Than Water*, appreciative fans were also copying the soundtrack and sending it along the bootleg highway.

Kim was happy to have Johnson back home; if for no other reason than the fact that he tended to turn very domestic after a long period away. She could count on him making her breakfast every morning, doing a fair pass at cleaning the apartment and basically putting everything but her wants and needs on the backburner. However Johnson could not be content to sit around for too long.

Which may have been the reason why when he was approached to do his first real acting job in 1999's lightweight romantic-comedy *Nice Guys Sleep Alone*, he accepted. This tale of the titular nice guy who can't find love and romance, features Johnson well down the cast list as the friend of the friend named Woody. Although he had done no acting other than the primitive student films at UCSB, Johnson proved quite adept at handling lines and hitting his marks. But like just about everything else circling his universe at that point, Johnson treated the acting experience as little more than a lark and made it clear that he had no intention of pursuing it fulltime.

Johnson returned to playing live. Occasionally solo and sometimes with local musicians Morgan Alstot and Gio Loria, he played shows in and around the Santa Barbara area along with occasional excursions into Los Angeles for small club gigs. It was during these shows that these audiences heard Jack Johnson's original songs for the first time. Word of mouth was spreading steadily and Johnson had soon built what could be considered a sizeable fan base. Again it was being suggested by those in his inner circle that it was time to get a deal and cut an album. And whereas he had once dismissed those notions out of hand a couple of years earlier, now he was taking the idea seriously.

The idea was being fuelled by the occasional surf holidays to such far off places as France, Australia and Indonesia that were bringing the shy performer face to face with his growing popularity. What he discovered on those trips was that Jack Johnson bootlegs, by now in sixth and seventh generation tapes and CDs, had literally reached around the world. In places as far removed as the South of France and Durban, people were coming up to him and telling him how much they loved his music and his album. The irony of course being that Johnson had not recorded an album.

'It was trippy,' he recalled in *Hooked On The Outdoors*. 'It was like all these little seeds were being planted all around the world.'

Early in 1999 another filmmaking opportunity presented itself. Kelly Slater had decided to get into the filmmaking game by producing a surf documentary called *The September Sessions*. The documentary would chronicle a one month trip to the famed Mentawai Islands, a string of islands just off the coast of Sumatra and in the middle of the Indian Ocean. An area considered by surfers in the know to have some of the best waves in the world.

Along for the ride would be the surfing stock company of Kelly Slater, Rob Machado, Shane Dorian, Brad Gerlach and Ross Williams. Emmett Malloy would edit the film but this would be a Jack Johnson production from the word go.

Johnson was faced with a hard choice. Chase music stardom or follow the surf? Johnson chose the latter.

'I was making surf films so you really couldn't ask for a better job,' he told the *Oakland Tribune*. 'I was travelling the world, going to islands in the South Pacific and spending a month at a time on these surf trips. Then I'd come home and would be working on the editing and putting these films together which was really fun too. So I kind of had the dream job. For me, that was as much fun as I could be having.'

But his decision was not made without temptation being thrown in his path. His surfing buddy Plunier had been given a copy of Johnson's songs and was so impressed with what he heard that he approached Johnson about going into the studio and cutting an album. Johnson was grateful for the offer but his loyalty to Slater and *The September Sessions* project made a recording session at that time out of the question. As it happens, Plunier was also about to get busy on some other projects. However the pair agreed to get together when things were a little calmer and see what developed.

The September Sessions shoot would be much more relaxed. Johnson was more confident in his filmmaking skills and the atmosphere in general was much more laidback. Johnson and his all star-troupe would get up in the morning when the sun was high and shoot for a few hours. During a lunch break, Johnson would catch a few waves until his friends were ready to surf again. Then he'd pick up the camera and get back to business.

Although he would inevitably miss Kim, Johnson was finding these around-the-world film excursions to be therapeutic. They allowed him the opportunity to surf the best waves in the world and, of equal importance, they fed his desire to get away from annoyances like telephones and real world bits of business.

Like the previous trip, *The September Sessions* shoot was conducive to songwriting. Easily the most memorable song to come out of the trip was 'F-Stop Blues', a song that Johnson has sheepishly said does not mean that much to him and was the result of some words that popped into his head.

With the conclusion of filming *The September Sessions*, Johnson returned to Santa Barbara and once again began editing. The resulting film was, by degrees, a little warmer and a little gentler outing. But like its predecessor, *The September Sessions*, requisite big waves aside, is a very humanistic film, sublime in its simplicity and an exciting journey into the lives of men who challenge the sea.

Jack Johnson had two films under his belt. The trips had been wonderful but he was making very little money off the projects. Johnson was about to turn to music.

06

The Music Starts Now

While Jack Johnson was contemplating his next move, his four-track missives to friends were continuing to make the rounds. His songs were reportedly the life of many a college town party in places as far afield as Texas and Florida. Further around the globe, his music could reportedly be heard on the beaches and inside thatched huts in Indonesia and Australia.

Friend and producer J.P. Plunier was blown away by the tape and passed it on to one of Johnson's idols, Ben Harper. Over the years Harper had been deluged with tapes by countless hopefuls hoping his blessing would put them on the fast track to stardom. In recent years, Harper had become burned out on listening to these unsolicited offerings and now rarely took these musical gifts too seriously.

But Harper thought enough of his producer and manager's taste in music to put on Jack Johnson's music. He was impressed with what Johnson was doing. He loved the idea that, while Johnson had clearly borrowed from several influences, including himself, the result had been an original voice. By the time he had listened to the tape several times over, Ben Harper emerged a real fan.

He told Plunier that he would like to meet Johnson. Subsequently Johnson was extended an invitation to meet Harper backstage at a show during a California date on his current tour. Needless to say, the young singer-songwriter was extremely nervous at the prospect of meeting one of his most important musical influences in the flesh.

The night of the show, Johnson sat transfixed as he watched Harper mesmerise his audience with an inspiring set of folk and blues. The humanity that came through on Harper's albums was there in the live setting; alternately powerful and inspirational and wrapped up in a totally humane and caring presentation. Johnson saw in that performance exactly the kind of performer he wanted to be.

Johnson went backstage after the show and was introduced to Harper. There was an immediate rapport between the two men. Like Johnson, Harper was a friendly, quietly outgoing person who gave off the vibe of not letting celebrity go to his head. He was quick to compliment Johnson on his music and, in subsequent meetings, he would regale the young man with tales of life on the road, the recording studio and the myriad ins and outs of the music business. Harper also took every opportunity to encourage Johnson to get into the studio and record as soon as possible.

Johnson was encouraged that no less a personage than Ben Harper was telling him that he should take the next step. But Johnson knew that next step would be a big test of his insecurities.

The reason being that Jack Johnson, even as he emerged from his musical cacoon, was still operating largely in a comfort zone. The musicians he played with were either close friends or fellow surfers. He had an aversion to even considering session musicians or players much more seasoned than he was and the overriding reason was the fear that his sound would somehow be compromised.

However, through what can best be described as friendly persuasion on the part of Plunier, Johnson had come to consider other options. The first person through the door of Johnson's brave new musical world was drummer Adam Topol.

Topol, born in Lake Tahoe, California, was a true student of drums and percussion, having spent three years learning the intricacies of his instruments at the prestigious Berklee School Of Music. After graduation, he travelled to Cuba where he spent six months continuing his musical education and learning the ins and outs of Afro-Cuban rhythms and beats. A much in demand session player, Topol's discography is highlighted by the albums *Culver City Dub Collection* and *Ritmo y Canto*.

Musically Topol was more than up to the task of playing with Johnson and it certainly did not hurt that Topol was both a good friend of Plunier's and a surfer as well.

But as always, Johnson was cautious. After all these years of isolation and informal solo performances for friends, the performer felt just a bit uneasy at the prospect of actually meeting another musician and actually playing his music with him. But Plunier kept insisting that Topol was a good guy and that he was a surfer. And so Johnson finally put two and two together and agreed to meet him.

When they finally did meet, the pair clicked instantly. They shared a love for the same kind of music and Johnson was excited at the possibilities that Topol's Cuban roots style of playing would bring to his music. For his part, Topol developed an affinity for the simplicity of Johnson's music and felt there was much he could contribute to it.

The next couple of months were a feeling-out process as the duo played a series of club and surf festival gigs for little or no money. Johnson was happily surprised to discover that Topol's diversity was adding texture and depth to what, to Johnson's ears, had been simply-structured songs that often sounded the same. Of equal importance was that Topol was obviously into the music and not just a mercenary looking for a job.

'Suddenly I had a musician,' recalled Johnson in a *Honolulu Weekly* interview. 'All of a sudden I had this guy who made me feel that my songs were worth playing.'

A couple of months into the try-out, Topol returned from a session for a Latin-jazz album, raving about this bass player named Merlo Podlewski. Podlewski, by way of New York City and Virginia, was a consummate, unassuming professional; more interested in keeping a song together than playing a flashy solo. This all sounded good to Johnson who invited the bass player down to play. His good luck with Topol did not prepare him for the slightly sceptical player who showed up.

The first words out of Podlewski's mouth were, 'I don't really like singer-songwriters,' he related in a *Daily Nexus* article.

Which was fine because neither did Johnson. In fact, while he was a singer-songwriter, he had never been a prima donna who expected his songs to be a certain way. Most importantly in his relationship with Topol and Podlewski, he never looked upon supporting musicians as mere sidemen but rather as integral parts to the overall creative process. Podlewski liked what he heard of Johnson's music and, more importantly, he liked his attitude. The bass player agreed on the spot to join Johnson's band.

The trio began playing out and the promise shown in rehearsals had almost instantly evolved into pure chemistry. Johnson's willingness to let his musicians interpret his music any way they saw fit was paying dividends. Johnson would present his songs as simple acoustic outings with an occasional blues tinge. Topol and Podlewski would respond with everything from a rock hard reggae beat, to bossa nova rhythms to a percussion heavy Latin-Cuban backing and the result would be full bodied compositions. For Johnson, the process 'was all cool.'

As Johnson became more active on the music front, with an eye toward going into the studio in the not-too-distant future, he was also, unexpectedly, about to get his first taste of stardom. Thanks to another surfer-musician who happened to front, in Johnson's estimation, one of the hottest bands in the land.

Garrett (G Love) Dutton of the band G. Love & Special Sauce and Jack Johnson had formed a mutual admiration society without ever having met. Johnson had long been a fan of the band and had incorporated some of the band's music into the soundtrack for *Thicker Than Water*. Dutton, an avid surfer who did most of his wet work on the waves off the New Jersey coast, liked Johnson's films. And so when Dutton, a Philadelphia native, came to Los Angeles to record in 1999, it was arranged, through skateboard filmmaker Scotty Sowens, for the two to meet up at Topanga Point near Malibu and do a bit of surfing.

The duo and some friends surfed for a couple of hours and then hit the shore. Dutton noticed that Johnson had brought his guitar with him and suggested that the two mix it up musically. In what was to be an hours long jam session, Johnson and Dutton exchanged songs they had been working on and played together.

'It was cool,' recalled Dutton of that day in *Hooked On The Outdoors* magazine. 'We just started trading songs. He played the song "Rodeo Clowns" and I kept telling him to play it over and over again.'

The reason being that Dutton was literally blown away by the song and the ease and naturalness in which Johnson delivered it. To say the least, Dutton was impressed with Johnson's songwriting skills.

The opportunity to spend the day surfing and playing music with one of his major influences had been a thrill for Johnson. He was even more thrilled when he got home and discovered a phone message from Dutton, asking if he would like to come down to the studio and jam some more.

Johnson met up with Dutton the next day at Topanga Point and the pair surfed for a couple more hours before driving down to the studio in Hollywood where the band was recording. What began as an afternoon session ended up going well into the evening with Johnson and Dutton playing along to their respective songs. Johnson was excited at the prospect of getting this insider preview of much of the material that would be on G. Love & Special Sauce's next album.

During the session, Dutton asked if he could record a version of 'Rodeo Clowns' with him. Johnson readily agreed, thinking it was an honour to have Dutton record a one-off version of his song even if it never went beyond the confines of the studio.

Unbeknownst to Johnson, Dutton played the rendition of 'Rodeo Clowns' to his label and the consensus was that the song had to be on the album.

'I took the demo of "Rodeo Clowns" to my producer T-Ray. Who did a lot of that Cypress Hill stuff and a bunch of old school hip-hop,' he told *Transworld Surf*. 'He was feelin' it and I was feelin' it and so we decided to ask Jack if we could put it out.'

The next phone call Johnson received from Dutton was the equivalent of the perfect wave. Not only did he want the song to be on his album but his label had strongly suggested that 'Rodeo Clowns' be the first single.

'We asked Jack, "Yo, can we cut this song?", Dutton told *Transworld Surf*. 'He was all "How about we cut it together?"'

The session for 'Rodeo Clowns' was much in the spirit of the previous day's jams. Dutton and Johnson worked easily together. If there was any pressure at all, it was on Johnson who was about to have his first song on an album released by a major label. But Johnson remained, outwardly, laidback in this tentative first step into the pop music world.

G. Love & Special Sauce's album, *Philadelphonic*, was released in mid-1999. Jack Johnson suddenly found himself very much on the pop music map. The single 'Rodeo Clowns', complete with G. Love's intro 'I got my man Jack Johnson in the studio today' became an instant addition to a number of FM and alternative-college radio stations. The song was a particular hit on the west coast where Johnson's films and live performances had made him the darling of the surfer-college set.

One of the first radio stations to throw its considerable weight behind 'Rodeo Clowns' and Johnson was XTRA-FM in San Diego, California.

Long a station willing to take a chance, several of the station's disc jockeys took an immediate shine to 'Rodeo Clowns' and put it into regular rotation on their playlist.

With the song's success came the first wave of major label interest in Johnson. Johnson knew little about 'taking meetings' and he was definitely not comfortable taking meetings by himself. And so, often with the closest thing he had to a manager at the time, Emmett Malloy, and long time friend Paul Gomez acting as his entourage, Johnson would wander into the corporate record company halls, dressed way down in T-shirt, shorts and sandals, to face the people who were eager for him to sign on with them.

By this time, Malloy had taken on a fatherly role in Johnson's business dealings. He was there to make sure that the fragile Johnson, when it came to business matters, would not be bulldozed. But truth be known, Malloy knew even less about the music biz than Johnson did.

Consequently, they would end up taking meetings with slicked back corporate label types that would often leave the admittedly naïve Johnson more than a little bewildered. For while he enjoyed the notoriety that 'Rodeo Clowns' was bringing him, Johnson was quite content to be squeezing out a living making surf films and playing the occasional live show. What the record companies were asking of Johnson seemed excessive.

Because Johnson had much simpler goals in mind. He was looking forward to some quality time with his girlfriend who had recently become his fiancé, going home to visit his parents at Christmas, surfing trips and more film projects. Johnson would listen to the record company speeches, often with his eyes glazing over, turn to Malloy for support and get the look back that said the decision was up to him.

During these meetings, Johnson and Malloy would often have to kick each other under the conference room table to keep from bursting out laughing at the seeming absurdity of the offers. Johnson would often liken them to the cliché of selling one's soul for rock and roll. He recalled that when questioned about whether he would be willing to give up filmmaking and, yes, surfing to go on the road to promote an album, he would look kind of sheepishly at the corporate executive and matter-of-factly say no.

'I was in a really nice situation,' he offered the *Oakland Tribune*. 'It wasn't one of those things I had been dreaming of my whole life and thinking "Okay, this is my big opportunity."'

It was at that point that J.P. Plunier and his partner Andy Factor came to Johnson with an offer too good to refuse: to be the first artist on a new label the pair was preparing to start called Enjoy Records.

Factor was a success story all his own. Starting out in the Virgin Records mailroom, Factor had worked his way up to the position of Vice President of A&R. He began working closely with Ben Harper and, by association, with Plunier. When Factor was asked to leave Virgin in 1999 during a corporate makeover, his last official act at the label had been to present Jack Johnson to the label to sign. Virgin said no to Johnson. Factor remained close to Plunier and the two actively conspired to do something at a later date that would reflect their easygoing, laidback sensibilities.

Factor had been paid a small royalty on Ben Harper's sales when he left Virgin and, in 2000, decided to put the money into having Plunier produce Jack Johnson's first album and release it on Enjoy Records. Johnson liked the idea of doing the album on an intimate scale, surrounded by friends. His ever modest thinking was that a Jack Johnson album might sell a few thousand copies to his fan base in the surfing world. Which was fine with Plunier and Factor who, likewise, had a modest projection for Johnson's first album; targeting it primarily to the shelves of independent record stores and surf shops.

Much like the progressive notions that guided his surfing documentaries, Johnson had some definite thematic ideas in mind for his first album. He felt the musical vibe had to be simple and unencumbered, free of effects and, to a large degree, overdubs. Johnson's feeling was that the album had to sound not much different than the backyard luaus where he first performed. Lyrically, his songwriting had remained simple yet socially and philosophically relevant and that was the attitude he would bring to the recording of his first album, *Brushfire Fairytales*.

'On the first album, the songs were all about the idea of how adults go to sleep watching the news,' explained Johnson in *Launch* magazine. 'News being a kind of adult version of lullabies. When you're an adult you watch the news and you hear about people dying.'

But while the intent of *Brushfire Fairytales* seemed sombre, Johnson has always maintained that his intent on that first album had always been good natured and mildly therapeutic. His mantra being that all people have the same problems and that his music makes people feel that they are not alone with those problems. Johnson's take as a lyrical psychiatrist was that his fans would feel better when listening to songs about someone who had gone through the same experiences and come out fine at the other end.

One song slated for *Brushfire Fairytales* seemed to run contrary to everything Johnson had intended for his debut disc, 'Bubble Toes'. On the surface the song seemed literally lighter than air and Johnson was the first to agree that it was nothing if not a trifle.

'That song's just a goofy love song that I wrote around the house,' he told *Launch* magazine. 'It's just sort of a silly little love song. My wife, she has some big fat toes, so I call her "bubble toes". It started out as just a little love song for her and then it's also got lyrics about any kind of person in a relationship.'

Well into 2000, Johnson, Topol and Podlewski had played together long enough to have transformed themselves into a tight musical ensemble. So much so that it only took them seven rehearsals to have the album's songs down and ready to record.

Brushfire Fairytales, recorded at Grandmaster Recorders / King Sound, was an exercise in speed and simplicity. Plunier ran an easygoing ship. The recording, in keeping with Johnson's laidback sensibility, was underproduced and gimmick-free. All of the album's instrumental tracks were recorded in three days. It took two more days to do all the vocals. The one expected addition was some steel drum work by Tommy Jordan on the song 'Flake'. But the big surprise came when Ben Harper, on a few days break from his current tour, showed up unannounced and offered to put some tasty slide guitar to 'Flake'.

God had created heaven and earth in seven days. Jack Johnson had created *Brushfire Fairytales* in the same amount of time.

'It was a lot of trust,' recalled Johnson of his studio relationship with Plunier in an interview with radio station 91X. 'It was really just a lot of us getting in there and doing it and bouncing ideas off each other. So much of my music was influenced by Ben Harper and since JP had produced him, we were pretty much on the same page. It really worked well. There was no time when we were on completely different pages. It was fun just to do it that quick.'

Within that time frame some real musical magic was created. In the studio, it was Johnson doing what he does best; playing melodic, simple guitar passages set against his trademark bluesy-folk vocals. But where the album, and especially on the songs 'It's All Understood', 'The News' and 'Posters', really stood out was in the way that Topol and Podlewski, with their Latin percussion and sly hip-hop lines were able to compliment and propel the songs far beyond the simple folk-blues idiom and into an arena that walked the line between simple and progressive.

The sessions were well planned out. But Johnson did manage to parlay a last minute studio notion into the song 'It's All Understood'. 'I wrote it in the studio when we were laying down tracks. I wrote the verses the day we were recording it and then the drummer and bass player came up with their own parts.'

Johnson had set out to make a very simple record and to a very large extent he had succeeded. Johnson's storytelling capabilities are very much to the fore on the album; simple lyrical odysseys that touch on the venerable touchstones of girls, hopes, wishes, struggle and happiness, all wrapped up in a leisurely island motif. Musically the album is uncomplicated. Structurally it is often delicate in form and tone.

As he would be prone to do in years to come, Johnson would quietly, introspectively, examine his just-completed album. He admitted that it made him nervous that silly love songs like 'Bubble Toes' would now actually be heard by, hopefully, millions of people. And he also expressed concern, in an interview with *Strand/China Business Weekly*, about exposing his personal feelings toward his wife and family in his songs.

'There's a balance,' he said. 'You want to say, "I'm not going to whore my personal life". But by writing these songs and putting them out, I already am. At some point I realised that it shouldn't change anything. I could write anything I wanted, like a journal, but then edit what I wanted to put on the record.'

The only certainty as *Brushfire Fairytales* stood poised for release was that the album seemed devoid of any commercial potential.

Johnson's songs did not fit into the prevailing musical formats of alternative rock, hip-hop and the pre fab boy and girl pop stars. The feeling was that the college crowd and surf devotees might make it a party favourite and that there would be a handful of low watt, risk-taking FM stations that would give the record a turn or two based on their memory of 'Rodeo Clowns'. But low expectations were the order of the day when *Brushfire Fairytales* was released on Enjoy Records in December 2000.

Reviews of *Brushfire Fairytales* tended to be mixed, with many journals, including *Rolling Stone*, simply dismissing the album as being too slight and inconsequential to be taken seriously. But many of the more learned and insightful publications saw through the slight veneer to something more substantial.

Q magazine applauded the album: 'It's laidback stuff, subtly melodious and really rather charming.'

Mojo magazine reported 'Johnson's songs are wordy and subtly funky. His voice sinewy...Cool.'

Uncut magazine stopped just short of an all out rave when it stated 'Johnson's sensitivity is authentic and there's a chilled freshness and a hip-hop lite inflection to his vocals.'

Not surprisingly, Johnson took both the good and bad reviews in his stride. Before the album even came out, Johnson had been advised from more than one person not to read his own press and he considered it good advice. The reason being that if the press was good, he would get a big head and that if the press was negative, he would get bummed out. It was a lose-lose situation and so Johnson chose to avoid the reviews altogether.

But in his quiet moments, he was optimistic at the album's chances. 'We had an idea that it might sell 5,000 copies,' recalled Johnson of his expectations for *Brushfire Fairytales* in a *North County Times* article. 'But when the album was getting ready to come out, we were suddenly expecting to sell maybe 20-30,000 albums if things went right.'

Things went right. A couple of influential FM stations jumped on 'Flake'. Word of mouth spread through the hotbed of Johnson support that an actual album was finally available. Sales raced past 5,000 in record time and were soon flirting with 20,000.

The early success of *Brushfire Fairytales* could once again be placed at the feet of XTRA-FM. Not long after completing the recording, Johnson personally sent a copy to the station. Johnson felt a strong connection to the city long before XTRA began playing 'Rodeo Clown'.

'I started putting my music in the soundtracks of my surf movies and the company that distributes the films (Moonshine Conspiracy) is from San Diego,' he said in a *Launch* magazine interview. 'There are a lot of surfers there. So San Diego was onto it before anybody else, just passing out bootlegs and things, friends just spreading the word.'

XTRA repaid the compliment and immediately picked 'Flake' as the song to play and other stations soon fell in lockstep and began playing the song as well. Johnson was amazed at the power the San Diego station seemed to have.

He was casting his fate entirely in the hands of the suddenly influential station. His team did not even bother trying to pick out songs that might work as singles. They reasoned that any song that XTRA went on would follow that example.

In the ensuing months, XTRA would pull out the songs 'Posters', 'Bubble Toes' and 'Mudfootball' and put them into their regular rotation, assuring Johnson of nearly non-stop airplay for the next six months.

Shortly after the completion of *Brushfire Fairytales*, Kim and Johnson were married, in 2000, in a simple ceremony on the beach of Santa Barbara. The couple took a leisurely month-long honeymoon before returning to their home base of Santa Barbara.

Johnson's good fortune would continue into 2001. *Brushfire Fairytales* was continuing to sell at a slow but steady pace. The latest round of offers from major labels was fielded and promptly ignored. Johnson and his band were playing increasingly larger venues up and down the California coast and selling out most of them. Johnson's film work was also beginning to gain recognition. *Surfer* magazine voted *Thicker Than Water* the best surf video of the year while his follow up, *September Sessions*, captured the prestigious Adobe Highlight Award at the ESPN film festival.

Johnson's friends, the Malloy brothers, were also catching their share of the brass ring. Their contributions to music videos and surfing documentaries had finally caught the attention of Hollywood and the pair were offered directorial duties on the motion picture *Out Cold*, a romantic comedy involving snow, snowboarding and nubile teens.

Just when things could not get any better, Johnson received an offer he could not resist. Ben Harper had 23 dates remaining on his current tour. Would Johnson be interested in opening for him? Johnson was knocked for a loop by the offer. He told *Guitarist* magazine, 'Making surf films was my dream job. But getting the opportunity to support Ben Harper on a tour through the United States and Australia seemed too good not to have a go at.'

07

Hit The Road Jack

It was a Chevy Astro Van. It had some miles on it. All the working parts did not always work when they were supposed to and it guzzled gas like nobody's business. But for Jack Johnson and his bandmates, it would be home for the next few months as they crisscrossed the United States and touched down briefly in Australia in support of Ben Harper.

Johnson was excited and cautiously optimistic at the prospect of going on the road. The up side was that he would be touring the country, playing his music and opening for his musical idol. The down side was one big question mark.

He would be touring in a big time concert situation for the first time and playing in front of hardcore Ben Harper fans who, with rare exception, had never heard of him or his music. Johnson would often admit in later years that his first tour with Ben Harper was one of the most nerve-wracking experiences in his life.

However from the moment he signed on for the tour, Johnson and his band were welcomed into the Harper camp with open arms.

It was at Harper's insistence that Johnson and his band would store their equipment in one of his vans. It was an unwritten rule that Johnson and his band were welcome to any backstage food. And when they could work it out logistically, Johnson and company could crash, usually on couches or on the floor, in Harper's suite of rooms. The kindness shown Johnson would stretch to include Harper's sound team who would freely assist Johnson during sound checks and work his sound during his set.

Johnson, Topol and Podlewski had long since jelled musically and it was much in evidence in those early shows with Harper. But the cross country trip in cramped quarters would strengthen their ties as people. Opening for Ben Harper was a classic example of paying one's dues. The members of the band would take turns driving, often all night and covering hundreds of miles, to make the next gig. It was cold and uncomfortable. Showers were pretty much out of the question for long stretches and so things tended to get a bit ripe. Rather than complaining, Johnson and his companions took it as one big adventure.

'I think the key is to pay your dues without realising you're paying them,' said Johnson in describing that first road experience in *Paste* magazine. 'When we were travelling in our little soccer mom van, the three of us took turns driving through the night to get to the next gig. And the thing is, we never once thought "Man, we need to get a bus." We were always just super-excited to be on the road with our friends, playing these little clubs.'

Johnson had no illusions about finding people at Harper's shows who were there to see him. But from that first show on, he was amazed to find a real sense of enthusiasm and warmth in the crowds he played for.

His lack of pretense, typified by the T-shirt, shorts and thong sandals he maintained as his performing attire, and shy demeanour was no doubt an attraction. The simplicity and sincerity of his set list, essentially the entire *Brushfire Fairytales* album, met with favourable response, with particular note being taken of the songs 'Flake' and 'Bubble Toes'. The aura of Jack Johnson on stage had become the ideal picture of laidback and friendly, something not too far removed from the performing stance taken by Harper. Audiences could not hate Jack Johnson if they tried.

'Ben's fans are real open-minded,' Johnson recalled of those early shows in an interview with the UCLA *Daily Bruin*. 'They just make you feel really welcome. The more shows I did, the more I realised that people actually wanted to hear me sing.'

As he would watch from the wings, Harper was also amazed at the response Johnson was getting from his fans. 'No one has ever been more embraced by our fans than Jack,' recalled Harper in a *Sports Illustrated* feature. 'He's reeled the surf culture back to his roots and is exposing a whole generation of kids to surfing's spiritual side. Everything about him is in perfect balance.'

Although he kept it to himself, Johnson, during those early shows with Harper, was battling nerves on an almost nightly basis despite having performed in front of audiences in small club settings. 'The way I feel when I first walk out on stage, I wouldn't be able to play music if I felt like that the whole time,' he explained to *Canoe*. 'It's always so surreal. I always sort of think, "How in the world did I get here?"'

Through shows in places like Minnesota and Ohio, Johnson put his time on the road to good use. When he was not performing or keeping up the mad pace to make the next show, he was soaking up every nuance of the road experience. The many hours spent with Ben Harper filled his head with stories of the road life, what to do and what not to do to get by in the music business and, most importantly, how a friendly, outgoing nature will serve one well in the long run.

'Ben took me on the road and just sort of helped me get along,' said Johnson in the *Honolulu Weekly*.

Johnson would later recall the tour did have its down moments. The most legendary being the night Johnson got sick and tossed his cookies on stage.

'I was on stage and I started thinking, right in the middle of the song "Middle Man," that I was going to throw up,' he laughingly recalled in an *MTV News* interview. 'I looked around and there was nowhere to go. The room was really packed and I couldn't really make it through the crowd fast enough. So I went and hid behind this pole and my brother (who had been travelling with the band for a few shows) passed me this beanie. It turned out it was Ben Harper's beanie. So I threw up in the beanie. Then I came back on stage, told the audience that I had just gotten sick and then went on and finished the set. Funny how you remember every little detail about things like that.'

It was not long into the tour that Johnson began getting reports from Plunier and Factor to the effect that sales of *Brushfire Fairytales* had jumped in every town he played in. By the time Johnson finished up his dates with Ben Harper, *Brushfire Fairytales* was flirting with 50,000 copies sold. Johnson liked the idea that his album was doing much better than anybody expected. However he was not looking too far beyond the dates with Harper which concluded in May 2001.

Johnson came off the road with Harper with some vivid memories of life on the road and of a lifelong friendship formed.

Johnson found the tour with Harper to be memorable on a number of levels. There were the simple moments of just hanging out with his idol, playing guitars and sharing songs. There was also the sheer joy of sharing the stage with Harper and playing in front of and winning over his fans.

Johnson had always looked at a music career as a kind of nebulous thing rather than something to be nurtured over a long period of time. His feeling was that he had accomplished his dream of playing with one of his musical influences, had made some money but that the ride was now over and that he would return to a life of movie-making and doing spot shows when he felt like it. He even had some thoughts of doing another album at some point. But Jack Johnson was not feeling especially career-oriented as he returned to Santa Barbara and the quiet life.

But his plans to retire from the music business was about to be cut short.

The response to Johnson's appearances with Ben Harper had been so positive that Harper's booking agent offered to book him and the band for a series of dates once his stint with Harper was over. And so after a short break back home to be with Kim and to get in some surfing, Johnson and the band once again hopped into the Astro Van and took off on a series of club dates that would last from summer 2001 until the end of the year.

Encouraged by his success opening for Harper, Johnson made a fairly easy transition to holding the spotlight by himself. Pre-show nerves were still a part of his performing routine and those privy to those early gigs agree that there was always a bit of shakiness in Johnson during the first song or two before he settled into his comfort zone. However, once there, the ease of his delivery and his believable sincerity proved a different kind of concert experience that audiences embraced.

As this second phase of live performing played out, Johnson began taking some liberties with his live show. He took what many would consider a risky move at some shows by showing his film *September Sessions* during breaks in the show. He would also keep audiences off balance by throwing in the occasional cover tune.

In their off hours, Johnson and the band had been playing around with the idea of throwing a Beatles song into the set. Once they settled on a song they felt would fit their vibe, audiences at Johnson's shows were surprised to hear an island flavoured 'Rocky Raccoon' or 'Don't Let Me

Down' dropped into the mix. Another cover hybrid added during those early touring days mixed music from blues legends Robert Johnson and Bo Diddley in with the Black Eyed Peas song 'Fallen Up'.

During his tenure on the Harper tour, Johnson had made the acquaintance of another singer-songwriter Mason Jennings. The pair became fast friends and would often end up crossing paths on the road and sharing the same stage. Devoid of anything approaching an ego, Johnson suggested that they alternate opening and closing the shows despite the fact that Johnson had a higher profile than Jennings at that point.

The reaction to those early shows, much like the present day, ran the gamut of emotions. Some audience members stood and swayed in time to the music. Others just sat quietly and listened. Still others appeared entranced in a dreamy state brought on by the island simplicity of Johnson's songs.

For his part, Johnson took a performing page from his mentor Ben Harper's book.

'We come out each night and every crowd is important,' he said in a 91X interview. 'We are never looking at shows as being stepping stones or looking ahead. We show up at a show and we are all really exited to play music that night.'

And what Johnson found was that his rabid fans, much like those who had followed the Grateful Dead, had taken to taping and trading his performances with other Johnson fans. Consequently an underground network of Jack Johnson's legions were creating an audio history of performances that began literally with his first appearances. Johnson had no problem with the tape trading phenomenon that had grown up around his music.

And, likewise, it did not bother him when unofficial bootleg CDs began being hawked along the internet superhighway and outside of venues where he played. The first known bootleg was entitled 'B.O.A.T' and consisted of the rough tapes of Johnson performing during the boat trip for the film *September Sessions*. A second fan-created bootleg, entitled 'J.O.A.T.' or 'Jack Of All Trades' was a collection of live performances, demo tapes and alternative versions of familiar songs. A third bootleg entitled 'Lullabies,' was similar in content to 'J.O.A.T.'

But to completely chronicle the exact number of bootlegs that had already been recorded and circulated would be an impossible task. By

2001, it was a safe bet that every show Johnson played was being record-ed by somebody in the audience. This was the time when downloading of songs on Napster and other song engines was hot news. But Johnson, who was still not convinced he had a career in him, was just grateful for the attention and amazed at the idea that anyone would want to go through all the trouble to record his music.

Through the summer and fall of 2001, Johnson toured almost con-stantly with the result being that more stations were jumping on *Brushfire Fairytales* songs and more CDs were being sold. While not overly con-cerned about the financial side of making music, Johnson could not help but be aware that the money for shows had gotten progressively better and that CD sales had reached and then surpassed the 50,000 mark, of-ficially putting the album in profit for all concerned.

But there were bumps in the road. Enjoy Records was still taking baby steps and would often stumble when it came to distribution and getting Johnson's album into the stores where Johnson was playing. On that mat-ter, Johnson would often express a mixture of bemusement and frustra-tion at having come to town and played a sold-out show, only to discover that his album was not in the stores.

Plunier and Factor were working hard to rectify the situation. They were also aware of the fact that, as the months went by and the album sales passed 75,000 and were well on the way to an unheard of, for small label artists, 100,000 copies sold, that the majors would once again come sniffing around.

Johnson's thoughts continued to be on everything but the bottom line. His overriding concern at the moment was that 100,000 people were now intimately familiar with the song 'Bubble Toes'. But as the spectre of big label interest began to enter his thoughts, he was expressing some concern about being the next pop star flavour of the moment.

'I knew I didn't ever want to be sucked into the music business ma-chine,' said Johnson in an interview with the *London Guardian Register*. 'I didn't ever want to be on the cover of *Rolling Stone* with my board pretending to be the next Beach Boy.'

But when the inquires came his way, Johnson was more than willing to hear them out. With Malloy fielding invites on his behalf, Johnson once again entered the hallowed halls of corporate music and he was not surprised when the offers seemed to be slight variations on what he had heard many times before.

Johnson recalled that the record labels would inevitably get around to wanting him to maintain the surfer image as a marketing tool but, in the same breath, would insist that he give up the very things that gave him that image.

'We'd sit with these people, kicking each other under the table, while they asked everything,' he recalled in *Sports Illustrated*. 'Do you do drugs? Do you always have a shaved head? Would you be willing not to surf, not to make films and to tour instead? Right there they'd shoot themselves in the foot. They had no idea what I was about at all.'

Johnson continued to tour, racking up sales and fending off offers from big labels. Finally, in late 2001, Johnson received an interesting offer from Universal Records. The company had come to Johnson with a totally fresh approach.

Universal knew absolutely nothing about surfing and surf culture. All they knew was that they wanted to be in business with him. Johnson played hard to get. Universal raised the financial stakes. Johnson refused again. The ball was in Johnson's court. What did he want?

Johnson's terms were simple. He did not want all the money in the world. He did not want Universal to dictate in any way, shape or form, the content of his music. It did not take long for Universal to blink.

Early in 2002 a deal was struck. Johnson would record his music and the music of any other act he chose under his newly formed label Brushfire Records. Universal would distribute his music but would only hear it when the album was completed and given to them. They would have no option to change anything about the songs, the artwork or anything connected to the music.

News of the deal with Johnson spread like wildfire through the music industry. Artists and executives alike were flabbergasted at the ease in which such a small, seemingly inconsequential performer like Johnson had managed to wrangle the kind of deal reserved only for the highest echelon of superstars from one of the biggest entities in the industry.

Universal had readily agreed to Johnson's terms and, by February 2002, he was already seeing the benefit of hooking up with a corporate giant. With the album now available everywhere, Johnson saw sales of *Brushfire Fairytales* climb to 130,000 copies, selling, at the time, an astounding 8,000 copies a week. The song 'Flake' continued its strong radio run, with Los Angeles radio station KROQ leading the way of rock heavy stations suddenly turning to Johnson's less-than-rocky style.

The reality of sudden stardom had left Johnson reflective in its wake. He was definitely making plans for the future. However, typical of Johnson, those plans were in keeping with his simple values.

The excitement level was such that Johnson was more than willing to play the role of musical troubadour for the next few years. But he was even more excited at the prospect of moving to Hawaii and raising a family.

The singer also chose easily the busiest time in his professional life to indulge a couple of quick side projects.

He zoomed in and out of the cinematographer's chair once again to shoot a video for the Foo Fighters' 'Breakout'. And when old buddy Taylor Steele was looking to round out the soundtrack to his latest surf documentary *Loose Change*, Johnson offered up his songs 'Middleman' and 'Mud Football' to the cause.

It was during 2001 that Johnson's growing reputation and circle of musical friends landed him a call for some creative help from the reigning hip-hop group the Black Eyed Peas. Long an admirer of the group, Johnson was admittedly curious as to how his mellow style might be of use to a group that was always high energy. But for the song 'Gone Going', Johnson's subtle playing and vocalising were the perfect tool.

Group member Will I Am recalled in a *Rolling Stone* interview that the pair worked on the song and then kind of put it aside. But four years later he resurrected the song for the album *Monkey Business*. 'We looked at it, put it on vinyl and scratched it and treated it as a sample.'

For the first time, Johnson was feeling the full impact of his success and he was ambivalent about it. During a turn through Los Angeles in 2002, where he would headline two sold out shows at the famed House Of Blues, Johnson told a reporter for the *Los Angeles Times* that 'This (the success) is so hard to figure out. I don't feel I deserve any of it.'

Playing the shows was not what was bothering Johnson. What was troubling was Johnson literally being overwhelmed with the non-music duties that went along with his big-time status. Photo sessions and the, by now, seemingly endless interviews were beginning to take their toll on the shy singer. With Malloy running interference, Johnson could pick and choose what he would do and, while agreeable to just about any duty, he would inevitably reach a point where he would say 'I don't want to do it anymore.' At that point all press and public relations would come to a halt until the singer was of a mind to start up again.

While in Los Angeles, Johnson drew a line in the sand when he blew off a scheduled meeting with Universal executives because he wanted to spend the day in Santa Barbara with his wife and do some surfing. The executives did not like it but they had no choice but to reschedule the meeting.

Johnson acknowledged the digging in of his heels when he told a *Los Angeles Times* interviewer, 'There may be a point where everybody's saying that it's a perfect time to promote a record and I may say it's a perfect time to chill out. I'll only do this as long as it's fun.'

As if to underscore the fact that Johnson was only into the music for kicks, he took some time off to go on a surfing trip with his friend Emmett Malloy that resulted in Johnson riding the waves in the movie *Shelter*. It was also during this filming that Johnson once again took some time off to surf and play, as part of the Sprout House Band that would end up supplying much of the music in the surfing documentary *Sprout*.

Johnson would revel in these kinds of moments when he could once again be just one of the guys and not bare the entire weight of a project. While the consensus was that these fun jobs would become rare with his growing success, Johnson insisted that he would always be available for something that would be no more rewarding than a fun time.

Johnson's indication that his burgeoning career could end at any moment ultimately proved an idle threat. In fact his enthusiasm level at the time was so high that it fuelled a new spurt in songwriting as he continued to tour well into 2002. Johnson already had a lot of songs in various stages of development that did not come close to making *Brushfire Fairytales*. Some he had put aside for a while and then returned to. Others were created during the endless one nighters that had opened up new sights, sounds and influences that were finding their way into new songs.

'I guess some people actually sit down and write,' he told *Launch*. 'I just never do that. I've always just written songs when they come naturally.'

With his elevation to headline status and the correspondingly longer sets, Johnson was forced to introduce new material into his set list. He was encouraged by the response to the new material and would keep putting out the new songs as the tour progressed. By the time Johnson began thinking seriously about recording a second album, all but three of the songs that would be on the CD *On And On* had already had a quite public airing.

But the first official product under his new Brushfire Records banner would turn out to be the soundtracks for his surf documentaries *Thicker Than Water* and *September Sessions* which Johnson, in the guise of producer, used his new-found knowledge of the studio to clean up what had been relatively primitive recordings and make them a little more high-tech on their way to a 2002 release.

Johnson now felt he was ready to record. In a perfect world, he would have liked Plunier to once again produce. But his friend was busy on another project and so the singer-songwriter cast about for another producer.

Mario Caldato Jr was a fast-rising young producer, having earned his wings on discs by The Beastie Boys, Beck, Los Lobos and John Lee Hooker. Johnson had initially rang Caldato up to do a remix of the song 'Posters' which at the time was being used in the soundtrack for the Malloys' motion picture soundtrack for *Out Cold*. Caldato was interested but felt the studio cut of the song did not give him much to work with. The ever-accommodating Johnson solved the problem by offering to come to the producer's house and cut a live version of the song.

The producer and musician cemented their relationship not too long after when Johnson decided to set up a studio in his parent's garage on Oahu. Caldato went to Hawaii and helped lay out with suggestions the specifics of the studio that would come to be known as the Mango Tree Studio.

'He said, "Man we should just turn this into a studio and just record the record here in Hawaii and have our families around,"' reflected Johnson.

By the time the studio was completed, Johnson had decided that Caldato should be the one to produce his next album. Caldato readily agreed, finding that the mellow vibe offered by Johnson was a welcome break from the often chaotic world of hip-hop and alternative rock that he had largely found himself in.

For his part, Johnson had no hesitation about having Caldato produce the album, despite the half joking-half serious suggestions that the hip-hop heavy producer might turn this mild beach bum into the new Vanilla Ice.

Johnson had done his homework and could tell by what he listened to that Caldato had spent a lot of time in Brazil and that he really understood the laidback beach culture of that country and its parallels to the Hawaiian beach flavour that Johnson favoured.

'He definitely isn't that one-dimensional,' he said in *Beat A Go Go*. 'I heard a bunch of stuff of his that was definitely not hip-hop.'

Caldato returned to Oahu during the summer of 2002 to produce the *On And On* sessions. Johnson has often stated that the nervousness he experienced when recording *Brushfire Fairytales* was not present this time around. He was recording in Oahu which added to his relaxed nature. They were not on the clock as with the previous album and, most importantly to Johnson's way of thinking, there was no pressure because he felt he had the songs.

Easily one of the standouts of the *On And On* sessions was the song 'The Horizon Has Been Defeated'. The song had been inspired by Johnson's vision of oil rigs rising up over the horizon off the Santa Barbara coast.

'We were pretty much finished with the album and we came up with this little idea right at the very end,' recalled Johnson. 'The scratch track was kind of reggae-ish and it went from there. Mario had been recording us while we had been working it out and we, literally, used the first (take) time we tried to play the song. I only had a few of the lyrics done and we went back and put those on afterward.'

Another popular cut on the album would turn out to be the song 'Taylor'. If there was a concession to commerciality on the new album, it would have to be this. Simple in concept and execution, Johnson had slowly fit the song into his live song list and it had proved quite popular even before the album was recorded.

Not surprisingly, recording in Hawaii dictated a leisurely routine. The musicians would rise at a fairly early hour and, according to Johnson in *Launch* magazine, 'use the day a little bit' and then go into the studio for a few hours. They would then take a break, usually as the sun was setting, and play music, surf or just hang out and then return to the studio for a few more hours.

'We spent a lot of time outside, barbecuing and just making it a family atmosphere,' he related in an *Oakland Tribune* interview. 'We were just putting ourselves in a situation where you forget what the ultimate outcome is; you know getting the album in stores and things like that. We were just kind of messing around, making music and having fun.'

Johnson recalled that having the family around would often result in interruptions in the process that were always welcome. He remembered the day that a particular gruelling session was interrupted by Caldato's daughter wandering into the studio, sitting down on the floor and playing. As the takes would unfold, Johnson would often be seen making funny faces at the little girl before they would both dissolve into laughter.

'He (Caldato) approached it the same way I was,' said Johnson in *Beat A Go Go*. 'Just wanting the family to be around, not to make it secluded or lock ourselves in the studio but to keep our lives the same and to record in the afternoon.'

Johnson remained very much a creature of habit and comfort during the sessions and felt the looseness of their lives had a big impact on the music.

'For us, it (the routine) worked out nice,' reflected Johnson in *Launch*. 'Our music is not very serious in a good way. I think it's about having a good time and I think it's important not to over-think the studio sessions. We all needed to be in a good mood and just kind of having a good time, first and foremost. So Hawaii worked out great.'

The game plan for *On And On* was literally a blueprint of the approach taken with *Brushfire Fairytales*. Johnson has insisted that he was not out to radically change anything on the new album. The *On And On* sessions were still a matter of Johnson singing and strumming his acoustic and Topol and Podlewski adding bass and drum rhythms as needed. But the presence of Caldato with his hip-hop and world music background proved a real asset.

'Mario definitely brought his own influences,' related Johnson in a VH1.com interview. 'He helped me get some nice tones and helped out on the subtle things like lyrical phrasing.'

Perhaps an influence of Caldato was the addition of more exotic instrumental underpinnings with streams of piano, accordion and melodica; courtesy of Johnson's old Santa Barbara buddy and Animal Liberation

Pipeline Beach, Island of Oahu, Hawaii
© Sean Davey / Surfpix 2000

Performing at Thunderbird Stadium, Vancouver, 2003
© Empics

With Jack's hero Ben Harper, 2003
© Michael Simon / Rex Features

Attending 'Bring Back The Beach' fundraiser, Santa Monica, 2004
© Marty Hause / Rex Features

With Perry Farrell at Surfrider Foundation gala, California, 2004
© Gilbert Flores / CPS / LFI

Jack in pre-Katrina *New Orleans, 2005*
© Empics

At the Curious George *world premiere, Hollywood, 2006*
© Gilbert Flores / LFI / CPA

Jack doing what he does best, riding a wave, Off The Wall, Hawaii
© Sean Davey / Surfpix 2004

Orchestra musician Zach Gill who flew over to the islands for a few days to lay down some tracks and do some surfing.

Gill and Johnson had stayed in constant contact since their Isla Vista-Santa Barbara days. Even after Animal Liberation Orchestra had relocated to San Francisco, they were constantly on the phone with each other. That Johnson was starting to gain some national and international recognition was no surprise to Gill, whose own band ALO was also doing quite well, albeit on a much smaller level. But his entry as unofficial member of Jack Johnson's band did come out of left field.

'He started inviting me out to play accordian with them on "Girl I Want To Lay You Down",' Gill said in a *Jambands.com* interview. 'We did that once at the Fillmore. It was really fun and totally rocked the Fillmore. Shortly after that he had me come out and do it at the Greek Theater in Berkeley. Then he was like, "Well if you're going to be down in Santa Barbara, why don't you do the Santa Barbara Bowl?" Then it was like, "Why don't you come out to New York and Boston?" So that's kind of how it began.'

While the basic bass, guitar and drums line-up had worked on the previous album, Johnson, felt *On And On* needed a bit more backbone. 'He thought, 'Maybe it would be fun to add some acoustic piano,' Gill told *Jambands.com*. 'So he just called me up and I played a little bit on the album.'

Caldato would later recall in an interview with *Mel In The Morning*: '*On And On* had a nice home feel and a nice vibe to it. The production work on the album was very simplistic but it was also tricky in that we also had to make it sound full with a lot less.

'What we were doing was very minimal but in the end it all boiled down to taste.'

Like his previous album, there was concern that *On And On* might be a bit too laidback to attain any kind of commercial success. Johnson was the first to admit that the first time he heard the album in its final form, it did sound a bit too mellow despite the steps taken in arrangements and studio polish. But one need only have looked at *Brushfire Fairytales*, which by the time *On And On* was completed had already sold in excess of 200,000 copies to realise that those fears were unfounded.

Truth be known, *On And On* was an advancement, albeit a quiet one. Johnson's playing is more assured on this album, throwing out many instrumental shifts and stylings. The odd electric moments are a welcome, taut and, aesthetically speaking, an appropriate leap from the previous album's straight acoustic line. Vocally Johnson is in top form; always expressive, sly and supple, wrangling just the right emotion out of each lyrical nuance. Topol and Podlewski dig much deeper into their third world and ethnic influences, providing sturdy and expressive backing.

Songwise Johnson has expanded his vocabulary. From the ecology-friendly 'The Horizon Has Been Misunderstood', to the philosophical 'Times Like These' to the songwriter at his wittiest in 'Wasting Time', Johnson has gone to the influence well and dredged up Ben Harper, Woody Guthrie and, if you listen closely, the ghosts of some long ago friends Dylan and Hendrix.

As it turned out, Johnson had heavier issues to deal with than how those first listeners were reacting to his efforts. For it was around the time that Johnson was recording *On And On* and readying its release that Kim announced, early in 2003, that she was pregnant. Johnson was overjoyed at the news and would find it hard to keep his mind on music with the prospect of being a father suddenly in his every thought.

Johnson would continue to tour throughout the rest of 2002 and into 2003.

It was at that point that the Jack Johnson Band became Zach Gill's high profile side project. 'When the album was done, we just started rehearsing,' he told *Jambands.com*. 'Originally I was just going to play in Australia and the US but then it was so much fun, I ended up going to Europe. So now I think I'm kind of in the band.'

And for Gill, it was a definite learning experience. He has acknowledged on several occasions that playing in front of 20,000 or more people on several shows with Johnson was a first for him. But he has also said that his primary concern during that first tour was to find his way within the band, to add what he could to the sound and to not be intrusive. He has often laughed at the fact that on that first tour the pressure was off his being the frontman because it was obvious that the audiences on that tour were not there to see him.

Understandably during this tour, Johnson made a point of never being too far from home or out for more than a few days at a time whenever possible. And when he was, he was on the phone to Kim several times a day.

The singer-songwriter sensed that he had reached the crossroads in a rapidly ascending career. Talk of the future still tended to make him uneasy and cautious. He knew there were pitfalls up ahead if here were not careful.

And Johnson was nothing if not aware of the fickle nature of pop stardom. Consequently he was fighting an internal struggle to stay the same person he was before choosing a music path and to not let the music change him. He was adamant in dismissing the music side of him as a weird side trip that he had the opportunity to explore but could leave it behind anytime he choose.

'I don't want to make myself think that I've got to start changing the sound because people are waiting for that,' he concluded in a *Beat A Go Go* interview.

But while he continued to waffle on the question of whether music was, at this point, his vocation or just a hobby with perks, one thing remained a part of his mantra; his humility in the face of his ever-growing success.

'I always feel really fortunate that I'm getting to play music,' he told a *Launch* reporter during his 2002 tour. 'It's something that I never wanted to force on anybody so it's been really exciting for me that people have been so behind everything I've been doing. If people weren't coming out to the shows I don't think I'd continue to try and play music live.'

As if to underscore the fact that Jack Johnson had not deprived him of his impulsiveness, during a short break in a packed 2002 touring schedule, the singer suddenly dropped everything and flew to the other side of the world to hang out and appear in a film being produced by his good friend Kelly Slater called *The Quicksilver Crossing*. Along with Slater and surfer-musicians Hans Hagen and Luke Monroe, Johnson was once again in his comfort zone as just one of the guys. But inevitably, when musicians of any caliber get together, jams happen.

Hagen reported in *The Quicksilver Crossing* that 'it was super having Jack on board. He set the pace, bringing everyone's music together.'

Likewise, Monroe, in recalling those jams, hinted of *Quicksilver Crossing* that 'We would be sitting there and Jack would be playing something. His new stuff is amazing.'

Johnson, on that trip, would acknowledge to *Quicksilver Crossing* that the trip gave him time to work things out. 'I was working on things that

I've been thinking about already or things that would inspire me down the track. I think there's a lot of experiences, such as scuba diving for the first time, that I'll be writing about later.'

His brief vacation over, Johnson hopped a plane, flew back to the states and that same night, was back on stage and back in business.

Johnson was finally beginning to see the financial fruits of his labour. The first residual cheques had been more money than Johnson ever could have dreamed of making off his music. Had he been more materialistically inclined, he probably would have indulged himself in fast cars and big houses. But this was Jack Johnson and so the indulgences would finally be in keeping with his simplistic outlook on life.

'The first thing I did was make a little recording studio and buy a place out in Hawaii,' he said in a *Billboard* magazine article. 'Because as long as I could end up here, everything was fine.'

08

Occupation: Musician

A lot had changed in just three years.

When Jack Johnson was going through airport customs in 1999 and 2000, he would have to declare his occupation. In those days, he would not hesitate to put down 'filmmaker'. But by 2001, the music side had kicked in and he was playing shows and selling albums. And so finally there came the day when, in the eyes of customs officials as well as his own, his job description changed.

'Then I had to mark down "musician",' he recalled in an interview with the *Ecucamonga Fansite*. 'All of a sudden that was my job. There was never really a step when it happened. It just faded that way.'

The reality that Jack Johnson had finally crossed over to working musician and budding superstar status officially kicked in in January 2003 when *Brushfire Fairytales*, thanks to constant touring on Johnson's part as well strong radio play and a healthy dose of Universal's distribution muscle, became the year's surprise story when it was awarded a platinum record for sales of more than one million copies.

Like just about everything else that the music industry had gifted him, Johnson was grateful, then amazed and finally humbled at the success of *Brushfire Fairytales*. He was at a loss to figure out how the fates had intervened on his behalf. But his contemplation of the big picture, like just about everything else in his life, was short lived. Then it was on to the more important things in his life. Family, friends and surfing.

Johnson had every intention of taking things easy into the new year, spending time with Kim and, when he could get back to Oahu, hanging with his family, long time friends and enjoying his every spare minute riding the Pipeline. The plans to permanently move to Oahu had taken shape shortly after the release of *Brushfire Fairytales*.

With his older brother Pete helping out, Johnson bought and refurbished a house not too far from his childhood home and a short drive to the homes of his brothers and their families. Like Johnson, the home was unpretentious.

Situated at the end of a long gravel driveway, the house sat on a gently rolling slope, seemingly carved out of the wilderness of tall standing palms. Adjacent to the property were two small guest houses, one of which Johnson would convert to the permanent incarnation of Mango Tree Studios. Inside, comfortable rooms led to a good-sized living room whose large window looked out into the sunshine.

Johnson had left paradise to find himself and the irony was that he had now returned to paradise to build a paradise of his own.

Johnson, who presented a very public image to the world, had pulled back to his childhood and his roots with the permanent move to Oahu. When he was not surfing or hanging out around the house with Kim, he would bike or drive the short distance to his parents' or brothers' homes and fall into an idyllic rhythm of simple island life and being in the bosom of family and friends. It was a simple mantra that Johnson, despite his growing celebrity, was steadfast in embracing.

It was not something that Johnson could easily put his finger on. As with just about everything in his life, Johnson could always find a spiritual, occasionally vague and very Zen-like explanation. He acknowledged it as there being a sense of specialness about being in a place where his whole family lived and good surf was only a short run down the beach. As with every other pronouncement, you either got it or chalked it up to not being on the same spiritual plane as the songwriter.

Musically, he was enjoying those quiet moments playing for his family and friends at quiet parties or beach luaus. For Johnson such moments had become rare, reminiscent of the times before music had become serious business and so he would savour every moment to its fullest. The singer had made some vague plans for some scattered west coast shows during this period and was always only a phone call away (should he choose to answer the phone) from any news his manager might have for him. But Johnson was obviously in relaxation mode as he waited for the projected May 2003 release of *On And On*.

'People are expecting certain kinds of things,' he said as the release date of the album loomed on the horizon in a *Honolulu Weekly* feature. 'People are either going to like it or think it's just too mellow.'

Johnson was not attempting to dodge the inevitable critical slings and arrows when he made defenses like that. It was just a matter of knowing his place in the pop music universe and, in his estimation, he would always be the prototypical outsider with his face pressed against the window of commercial acceptance. He felt that he could make himself crazy trying to figure out what moved people to buy his music or his concert tickets and, quite simply, that was not a road he chose to go down.

The singer's plans for a relaxing good time came to an unexpected end when Ben Harper called with the offer of some heavy duty touring plans to kick off the new year. The pair would start things off in March with a 13-date trek through Australia and New Zealand. They would then immediately return to the states for a series of joint outdoor appearances at a trio of massive outdoor festivals.

Johnson was excited to be heading down under. His previous shows in Australia had gone over well and, thanks to the tape trading underground that had grown up around his surf film music and the better than anticipated response to *Brushfire Fairytales*, the singer was assured of a strong reception. In fact, it was during those 13 dates that the first hints of worldwide Jack Johnson mania were being heard. Nothing to rival Beatlemania but, for its time, the fan and press attention was literally constant and overwhelming to the laidback singer. Johnson was grateful for the rock star attention but it was almost automatic at this point that the mild-mannered singer would avoid it at every opportunity.

Playing in front of enthusiastic audiences on the other side of the world was a potent elixer for Johnson. He had learned much on his previous brief trek to Australia about the people and what they responded to. While he never tailored his show to an audience, he was instinctively plugged into just what people in this blue-collar rough-and-tumble part of the world craved and his simple, straightforward non-pretentious approach was it.

Having played with Harper previously made the concerts a seamless exercise in styles mixing and matching into an enjoyable whole. Their similar styles and presentations blended effortlessly together into a concert experience in which the words mellow and meaningful played out in a constant acoustic fire.

A bonus for the performers was that they had hit Australia and New Zealand at the height of the surfing season. Consequently when there was a lull in tour activities and the endless round of press interviews, Johnson and Harper would grab their boards and head for open water. Unfortunately that tour found the surf to be far from exceptional which, recalled Johnson, was the only downside to his trip down under.

'Australia has that same kind of outdoor lifestyle that I grew up with,' he related in *Slap* magazine. 'I just really enjoy the culture.'

The two performers returned to the states in mid-April to begin the US leg of their tour with appearances at the aforementioned festival shows. The first, in late April, was at the prestigious two-day Coachella Valley Music And Arts Festival in Indio, California. Coachella is well known for its bringing together of a variety of non-related musical styles. Johnson had expressed some concern that, despite the festival's open door policy, his laidback style might not go down as well with the audience's modern rock sensibilities. He was happily surprised at the warm response his music received.

Coachella was followed by an appearance at the New Orleans Jazz & Heritage Festival, scant days before the release of *On And On* in May, and the second annual Bonnarro Festival in June in Manchester, Tennessee.

Upon its release, *On And On* proved an immediate smash. Unlike its predecessor, there was no gradual climb up the charts. Within a week of its release, the album was nestled firmly at number three on the national pop album charts. There was no reluctance on the part of radio stations to add the first single from the album, 'The Horizon Has Been Defeated', to their playlists. Critically, things continued to be a mixed bag for Johnson. Some publications took him seriously as an artist while, for a number of critics, his simplicity and distinctiveness continued to make him an easy target.

Rolling Stone continued to lead the charge of the barb brigade when it dismissed the album by saying 'It requires a leap of faith to trust that Jack Johnson is really that calm.'

Entertainment Weekly opined 'Johnson's songs are more instantly likeable than his jam band peers.'

Q magazine, previously supportive of Johnson, turned with a vengeance when it said 'Oh how it drags.'

E Online stated: 'It's sweet and kind of sexy but clearly designed for those who think John Mayer too challenging.'

Blender liked the album: 'Johnson pushes past folk and roots distressed interiors and glides into cool, new musical areas.'

As was his want, Johnson rarely looked at album reviews but, in a masochistic way, felt that he had to read every *Rolling Stone* mention. This particular review struck him as funny in a backhanded sort of way.

'The review said I couldn't possibly be this calm,' he told *Chicago Innerview*. 'But I'm not trying to come off as anything so I guess I am that calm.'

But like his previous album, when it came to his ever-growing fan base, *On And On* was critic-proof. It was an album universally loved and one that would sell a million copies in a year. But just after the album's release, Johnson, despite the rush of sales, was not hoping for too much.

'I kind of accepted that the success of the first album could have just been the flavour of the month,' he told MTV News. 'And it would have been still just as exciting and fun to me if this record came out and sold nothing. I would have just looked at that one as kind of this crazy thing that happened and it was a fun ride. But since this one's doing okay, I'm just going to keep rolling with it.'

Shortly after the release of *On And On*, Johnson was making plans to tour for the rest of the year. Initially he thought about going out with his friends, G. Love & Special Sauce, Donovan Frankenreiter and Mason Jennings. There was also the rumour being floated that his old surfing buddy and sometime musician Kelly Slater might open for Johnson for a handful of dates.

But again it would be Ben Harper, who had grown fond of life on the road with his young protégé, who once again rang him up with a tour in mind.

Johnson would go out with Harper for a series of US dates that would run through June and July. They would be billed as co-headliners. They would be travelling on buses rather than the Chevy Astro Van. Johnson was thrilled to once again be going out on the road with Harper for what was shaping up as an extended summer vacation. Johnson was never what one would consider a superstitious man but, when explaining to friends and reporters alike his feelings about his sudden run of good fortune, he would often stammer that it was all just good luck.

Things had changed a lot since Johnson had toured with Harper the first time. They would now be playing larger venues in the 5-15,000 seat range. The nature of the tour would allow Johnson to do a full set. Finally the success of two albums, a ton of radioplay and nearly two years worth of touring under his belt had moulded Johnson into a more confident performer who, on this tour, would become a true headliner.

Johnson's shows consisted of a generous helping of songs from his first two albums, the odd fragment of something new he had been working on and the occasional good time cover of everything from Jimmy Buffet's 'Pirate Looks At 40', Bob Marley's 'Stir It Up' and, as a nod to the master, Ben Harper's 'Please Me Like You Want To'. Sometimes Harper would appear on stage and sit in with Johnson for a song or two and the smiles and friendly nods that accompanied those moments when two friends creatively shared the stage were, in a word, priceless.

With a full set that often came in at just under two hours, Johnson was now in a position of being able to stretch out on certain numbers. Compact songs would often erupt into impromptu jams in which Topol and Podlewski would strut their stuff. Johnson's easy going performing persona would allow for audience participation and songs of quiet introspection would often evolve into light-hearted sing-a-longs with audiences in the thousands joining in at Johnson's urging. During the second Harper tour, Johnson would often project earnestness but at the end of the day his concerts were about one big party.

Johnson could do no wrong on the stage. Even those moments when he felt that something had not gone according to plan, an off-key vocal, a too strident guitar chord and, yes it did happen, the forgetting of a lyric, ended with his being greeted with spontaneous and heartfelt cheers and applause. Johnson had become the Teflon performer and he was at a complete loss as to why.

'The second you figure out what everyone digs about your music is probably a bad revelation because you'll start trying to move in a direction people want to hear,' he said in *Paste* magazine. 'Thankfully I'm not too concerned with trying to figure it all out.'

The tour with Harper was literally friction free. There were none of the often inconsequential things that often drive a stake into friendships.

Johnson and Harper would joke with each other, often ate and hung out together and would talk after a show well into the early morning hours. Harper and he had become Backgammon partners and could often be found hunched over the board for hours on end. Harper was still the mentor and Johnson the willing student but on this tour, they had emerged as equals.

Off-stage Johnson kept up the self-effacing image that had proved so endearing. When their schedule permitted, Johnson would often take the day to explore whatever town they were in. Sometimes on skateboard and often on foot, he would play tourist and see whatever there was to see. Despite the fact that he was now a widely recognised star, Johnson seemed to easily blend into his surroundings and could walk the streets without being noticed. When he was approached, Johnson was gracious in meeting his fans, accommodating with autographs and willing to just talk to people who would come away from those meetings amazed at the sheer humanity of the man.

Throughout the later portion of the tour, it had become an unwritten rule that Harper and Johnson would make token appearances, usually a song or two, during each other's set. But a late-in-the-tour stopover at The Greek Theater in Berkeley, California would prove a particularly heady night for Johnson.

Midway through Harper's set, a surprise guest was announced. Carlos Santana stepped out of the wings and sat in on the songs 'With My Own Two Hands/War' and 'Voodoo Child'. The atmosphere on the stage was electric for Johnson as he stood offstage, watching as two legends traded licks and vocals. Johnson was so amazed that, to him, it was almost an afterthought when he was brought on stage to duet with Harper on the song 'High Tide Or Low Tide'.

Following the conclusion of the Harper tour, Johnson returned to Oahu to spend some time with his wife, be with friends and yes, of course, to surf. It was during his return to the islands that Johnson moved as far away mentally and emotionally from the music business as he could possibly get. He would reflect on how what had come to him had come too big and too fast and, in his own mind, wished he could run away from it.

'Really, it's overwhelming,' he said at one point in 2003. 'At some points, I go "This is going to be the last tour that I do." I'd be just as happy a person if it didn't all happen. I tour for a month, playing in front of thousands of people, and, yeah, it's a real big buzz doing it. But when I come home and surf good waves for the first time and get to hang out with a couple of friends, I get happier just being back home with friends than I do from the buzz of a big show.'

Inevitably Johnson's love for the music would return. But to those handling Johnson's business affairs, and especially the corporate types at Universal Records, his comments were a reminder that Jack Johnson was not the stereotypical rock star who could be manipulated and that long term career plans could not be made. Because Johnson had gotten into the music business on his own terms and he would go out the same way.

Johnson returned to the touring wars in August with another jaunt across the Atlantic with stops in France and Japan. His reception in these countries continued the world wide Jack Johnson craze as sold-out shows and wildly enthusiastic fans remained the order of the day. There was no doubt that Johnson's message was universal.

Johnson found a particular affinity for the people and culture of Japan. 'There's a big part of Japan (in terms of culture) in Hawaii. When I was growing up, the big thing was to never wear your shoes inside the house and that's a big part of the Japanese culture. I found when I went there for the first time I just really felt at home and the people that I met there reminded me of friends I had back home.'

The European leg of the tour was fairly hectic with lots of one-nighters and lots of travelling in between. However things became much more relaxed when Johnson came back to the states. This part of the tour was more of a family affair as wives, girlfriends and family members would come along for short stretches of time. Kim was now fairly along in her pregnancy and had stopped working to devote all her time to being an expectant mother. Having her along put Johnson at ease. He was with her constantly when he was not performing and even when he was doing interviews or attending to other public relations necessities, she was never too far away. It was the first time Kim had seen her husband perform at this level and she was blown away at the size of the crowds and the level of response.

Watching from the wings, she was also amused when young women would scream out their love for her husband, shriek, swoon and throw their undergarments at Johnson's feet. Amused in the way Johnson would blush and aw shucks his way through the adulation.

Easily one of the most enjoyable moments of the 2003 tour was a swing through Los Angeles. Johnson headlined a sold-out show of 17,000 at the world famous Hollywood Bowl. It was typical of the way that the performer had come to transform even massive audiences into a good time party. From the last row, in which Johnson could only be seen as a speck on the stage, to the more privileged in the front rows, bodies were up and swaying with the first song. Johnson was at his best, quietly yet powerfully emotional, projecting even the most lightweight songs into statements of substance as Topol and Podlewski filled in the spaces with third-world purpose.

Much of Johnson's enthusiasm that night doubtless had to do with the fact that his parents, Jeff and Patti, as well as Kim had come over from Oahu to join the west coast leg of the tour. The smiles on their faces said it all. Jack Johnson had made his family proud.

While in Los Angeles, Johnson had agreed to make an appearance on the late night television show *The Late, Late Show With Craig Kilborn*. Johnson was a bit skittish about doing television, preferring to just play rather than engage in innocuous small talk with the show's host. But he made an exception because of the show's reputation for attracting a hip, young audience.

The day of the taping, the studio was packed to the rafters with ardent fans who had gotten wind of the appearance and had gobbled up most of the available tickets. In the back row, Jeff, Patti and Kim sat smiling. Backstage Johnson was smiling a nervous, anticipatory smile. Finally the show's announcer brought Johnson onto the stage. The audience rose to its feet with a standing ovation. Dressed in his trademark T-shirt, shorts and sandals, Johnson smiled as he moved to a stool at centre stage, guitar in hand. The crowd sat as Johnson muttered a thank you. He began playing out a low easy rhythm. Amid the hot lights and Hollywood glitz, he was comfortable.

True to his word, many of the shows that Johnson did in the latter half of 2003 were star-studded concerts featuring such heavy friends as G. Love & Special Sauce and Donovan Frankenreiter. The blend of those musical styles was infectious; with a myriad of musical elements combining to form the same party atmosphere. It was apparent to anybody who happened to see this group of friends perform that they were witnessing a changing of the guard. G. Love & Special Sauce were, by association, the grizzled veterans of the scene while Donovan Frankenreiter was the up-and-coming new kid on the block. As for Johnson, it was evident from the thunderous ovation that greeted his presence on stage that he was the once and future king of mellow music.

Johnson was also taking this transitional year to find himself as an activist. His earliest testing of those waters came as a teen when he was a member of the Surfrider Foundation. But he has admitted that was a rather benign experience, more an outgrowth of his surfing lifestyle than any abiding interest in preserving the planet.

But with age, Johnson had come to take a more active look at the planet and its people. Social and ecological concerns had started to take a more active role in his songwriting. The song 'The Horizon Has Been Defeated' being an all too plain stab at the state of the planet. While not overtly political, Johnson was also more than stating an opinion on the state of the union, with the later song 'Good People' a not too subtle shot across the bow at a society and a people who had elected George Bush president.

'I'm not someone who grew up thinking of things in a green way,' said Johnson in a recent interview with *The Surfer's Path*. 'It probably came about when I realised that what I was saying and what I was doing were being heard and thinking about kids and the effect it had on all of them. That made me start thinking about what I could do in a positive way. '

What he did, quite simply, was incorporate his attitudes into his performing life. In interviews conducted in 2003, he would talk at length about how his album sleeves were made of recycled paper. His US tour buses and equipment generators were being run on biodegradable diesel fuel and he made a point, with the aid of a recycling coordinator, to encourage those around him to clean up and recycle after each of his shows. The year 2003 was also when Johnson was introduced to the organisation 1% For The Planet, an ecological group that strongly encouraged member companies to donate 1% of their profits to ecological causes. Johnson immediately signed on and became one of the group's most outspoken supporters.

'I had met Yvon Chouinard (1%'s founder) and was able to go on a few surf trips with him,' recalled Johnson in *Radar Report*. 'So I learned a lot about the organisation and how important it is. I thought it was a really cool way to help out and easy to do. I mean, who's going to miss one percent of their revenue?'

Johnson had always been modest about his philanthropic causes, saying on several occasions 'I always think of what I do as the bare minimum.'

In 2003 Johnson and Kim turned a charitable eye toward Hawaii and its ecological needs with the formation of the Kokua Hawaii Foundation. The Foundation, in turn, begot an annual all-star Kokua Music Festival whose proceeds would fund ecological and recycling programmes on the islands. Johnson would help out the cause on a personal front when, on his return to Oahu, he began going to schools and playing songs designed to get kids into a recycling state of mind.

He took particular pleasure in this aspect of his good works. It was something that was personal to Johnson and it was a cause that he could actively execute literally at his backdoor. As it grew, his foundation would number several lifelong friends which added immensely to Johnson's all important comfort zone.

While enthusiastic in his causes, Johnson would often acknowledge that he is walking a fine line when it comes to causes and, like celebrities that have taken up causes before him, he has to be careful.

'There's a balance I've been trying to find between speaking my mind a bit and still being kind of a lazy surfer,' he has said in *The Surfer's Path*. 'I want to speak my mind but I don't necessarily want to be a spokesman on things like politics because I don't know every fact and everything that's happening. But when it comes to the ecology and the future of this planet, I guess I am pretty passionate about it.'

Johnson took one more trip to Australia in November that effectively ended his touring for the year. He returned to Oahu in time to spend a quiet Christmas with his family and friends. It was once again a time of reflection and looking to the future.

Because the days were counting down to the moment when Kim and Johnson would become parents.

09

The Family Way

Moe Johnson came into the world in February 2004. It was an uneventful delivery. Mother and baby doing fine. Father in a state of euphoric shock. Outwardly there was not a happier man on the planet. Inwardly, 30-year-old Jack Johnson was now at peace.

Starting a family on the island of his birth, surrounded by loving family and friends; Johnson was alternately ecstatic and teary-eyed as he drank in every precious moment of the miracle of life. In his mind the birth of his son was symbolic of the cycle of life and its meaning to him. The torch had been passed to the next generation. Jack Johnson's life was now complete.

Needless to say, everything connected to music was immediately put on hold. Everything pertaining to the business side of Johnson's music was handled by Emmett Malloy who knew better than to bother Johnson with anything but the most extreme emergency. And even in those rare instances when his manager felt it necessary to call his charge, he was inevitably greeted by the trademark Jack Johnson phone message that said 'Leave a message and I probably won't get back to you.' A message that indicated in no uncertain terms that he did not want to be bothered.

Chris had heard that message before but, instinctively, knew that fatherhood was something that Johnson wanted to savour in a pure, isolated way. And so Malloy relayed Johnson's edict to everyone from well-wishers to record company executives. His charge was simply not available. And just about everybody understood.

In the days and weeks that followed the birth of his son, Jack Johnson sailed easily into the role of doting husband and father. He beamed the day he changed his first diaper and, with friends, would laughingly speculate on when, like his father before him, he would take his son out on the surf for the first time.

As always, he was totally attentive to Kim's needs. The bond between them had only deepened with the birth of their son. Kim had always come across as being cut from the classic earth-mother mould; strong and independent in her own right and totally committed to family. These traits were much in evidence during those early days of motherhood as Kim instantly bonded with her son.

Johnson would often hover in the background, watching as Kim and Moe played or slept. His sense of family and the joy of it playing out in front of him had burned deep into his heart and soul. The man-child persona that had carried him to this point had, in Johnson's mystical world view, taken a giant step into adulthood.

Johnson was very much the landed gentleman during those early days of fatherhood and those around him were quietly amused at his turn in attitude. He would wax enthusiastic about such seemingly mundane topics as the nearby compost heap and the fruit trees that bordered his property.

Johnson had always been an avid skateboarder and most days would find him riding up and down the gently winding roads that dotted the island. Johnson was easily at his most competitive when it came to the game of ping pong. He had long ago built what he called his 'Ping Pong Room' where a regulation sized table became the battleground for Johnson to take on family and friends in extremely spirited games, most of which were inevitably won by Johnson. The 'Ping Pong Room' is also where nearly all of Johnson's gold and platinum record awards ended up hanging. To Johnson the awards meant little other than the fact that there were so many of them that they were beginning to clutter up the house. So finally, in a bit of housecleaning, they all made their way out of the main house and onto the walls of the Ping Pong Room.

He would always find time to surf and would use the time riding the waves at Pipeline to contemplate the wonder of it all. There was a sense of deep thought and contentment as he rode the waves or sat safe and secure on the shore. It was not, as he was prone to admit, unlike the winding-down period after a long tour. Whether riding the best Pipeline had to offer or simply strolling along the beach with his family or friends, Johnson's sheer joy at experiencing the life he chose was very much from a Zen place.

Johnson would be the first to admit that his head was now in a very mellow place, a place that would most certainly impact on the rest of his life and career.

During those early days, he hardly gave music a thought. But with the influx of new thoughts and feelings, it was inevitable that those thoughts would be channeled into his music. Idle moments would find Johnson plucking his guitar and playing with lyrics while sitting alone on his parents' front porch, staring out at the waves crashing onto the shore.

He was particularly fixated on the view of legendary Pipeline and acknowledged on several occasions that this simplistic picture of nature at work was a constant creative influence.

When he did begin to think about his music and the fact that he would have to tour again at some point, his heightened sense of family played a big part in his decision making. Johnson had acknowledged that he had been touring quite a bit over the past three years. But now, in deference to his wife and newborn child, he was determined to limit touring in 2004 to no more than two months. And, in a mutual agreement that had been brewing for a while, Kim would give up teaching to devote her time to handling much of Johnson's day to day business affairs. Kim was quite happy to be taking on the full-time role of wife-mother-manager. But Johnson recalled that it was not a decision that sat well with his inner circle.

Friends and professional acquaintances alike had told Johnson in no uncertain terms that having his wife involved in his business could have a negative effect on both his personal and professional life. But Johnson chose to ignore those sentiments, indicating that he would rather not do music at all than have it take him away from his wife.

Johnson was continuing to find comfort in the fact that his business dealings were looked after by a close-knit circle recruited from a group of life-long family and friends.

'Everytime we think we're going to have to hire a stranger, something magical happens,' Kim recalled to the *Honolulu Weekly*. 'Someone we know shows up with experience in that area, we find a way to solve the problem. It hasn't failed us yet.'

Johnson was also using his down-time to expand his Brushfire Records roster. While the label was already profitable with Johnson, the singer felt it was aesthetically and creatively sound to have other acts under the Brushfire tent. And it was not like Johnson would have to go beating the bushes for musicians willing to sign on the dotted line.

At the point where Johnson became a 'name' on even a moderate level, he was dealing with submissions from hopefuls aiming to land a deal with him. He would be the first to acknowledge that those submissions ran the gamut from good to dreadful. But when signing new acts became a priority, Johnson was going to be selective. He would not be the typical A&R man trawling the clubs and sifting through tapes hoping for a surefire hit. His criterion had always been to sign people he liked personally as well as musically. The recurring theme of keeping a tight circle of friends around him at all times once again being in evidence as he thought about who he'd like to hang with.

His first official addition to the Brushfire label was made easy when G. Love & Special Sauce came to a parting of the ways with their previous label. Johnson immediately stepped in and signed his old friend who had given him his earliest success. And while his friend Zach Gill's band Animal Liberation Orchestra was not immediately brought aboard, there was an unspoken promise that the band would eventually fall under the Brushfire banner.

Donovan Frankenreiter recalled taking the initiative in his quest for a deal with Brushfire. He had known about Johnson's label for quite some time and, when he felt the moment was right, he sent his friend a demo. Given their friendship and touring history, it was no surprise when Frankenreiter heard back from Johnson saying, in essence, 'Come to Hawaii and let's make a record.'

Johnson co-produced Frankenreiter's album with Mario Caldato Jr. Johnson contributed vocals, guitar, bass and ukulele to several tracks. Feeding the session were G. Love and members of Ben Harper's band who would drift in and out of sessions, offering instrumental and vocal support. And like previous Johnson albums, Frankenreiter's album, recorded at Johnson's Mango Tree Studios, was seemingly more fun and games than real work.

'There was no pressure,' recalled Frankenreiter in a *South Florida.com* interview. 'No one was yelling, "Hey. C'mon I don't hear a hit!" We just surfed, hung out on the beach and jammed. When we were done, there was a record.'

Recording G. Love's album *The Hustle* was almost a carbon copy of Frankenreiter's experience. Although his band members remained with him, G. Love had decided to drop the Special Sauce from the band's name. The resulting session, again produced by Mario Caldato Jr, allowed Johnson the luxury of playing guitar and adding occasional vocals and just hanging with a good friend.

Dutton recalled that signing with Brushfire Records was the best creative thing to happen to him in years and that the ease of his relationship with Johnson remained during the recording of the album.

'When we went into the studio we were told to keep it simple, keep it raw and just do what you do,' he recalled in a *Glide* magazine interview. 'We were told to not try and make a radio song. It was a place where we finally had the confidence to go in and record live again and to have a producer that was able to make the music jump off the stage.'

All this helping out on other people's albums was definitely putting Johnson in the frame of mind to record again. Much like his previous outings, the singer did not have a masterplan for recording what would become the album *In Between Dreams*. But his current state of mind would be a factor.

Unlike the vibe present in *Brushfire Fairytales* and *On And On*, Johnson, with the birth of his son and the increased sense of well being that went with now living permanently on Oahu, was not inclined to use his latest batch of songs for social commentary as much as he was inclined to celebrate the sheer joy of being in the world. Thus the notion behind the songs for *In Between Dreams* was, even by Johnson's own standards, extremely simple.

'Instead of thinking about things that have been pissing me off, I've been thinking a lot about family,' he said in an interview with radio host Brian Barnes.

But family in a philosophically deep, somewhat surreal way that would appear to reimagine classic philosophers in a pop music setting. In the past, there had always been references made to the fact that Johnson's more progressive songs had been influenced by his days in film school and the constant exposure to Goddard and Kurosawa films. There was also a sense of deeper thinking in the songs destined for the new album.

'We toured a bit after the last record and I take in a lot when I'm in different parts of the world,' he said in explaining the concept behind the new album to *Billboard* magazine. 'So when I got back home, I had time to gather my thoughts and get back to my normal life. That's the idea for the title. Those adventures that I go on now, sometimes I feel like I dream them. All the tours and shows are a lot of fun but it's a different reality.'

Johnson was not tied to any kind of rigid schedule when it came to recording *In Between Dreams*. From a pure dollars and cents point of view, Universal would have liked another album in 2004 to capitalise on Johnson's worldwide popularity. But Johnson could not be rushed into the recording process and so Universal and everybody else in the real world would simply have to wait until the singer felt like it.

However Johnson was not oblivious to the realities of the business. He knew that, even with a truncated schedule, he would have to do some touring in 2004. Ultimately the decision to record *In Between Dreams* in the summer boiled down to a short-list of very simple requirements. Mario Caldato Jr, who had rapidly ascended to the position of in-house producer for all Brushfire artists, would once again helm the console. The album would be recorded in Mango Tree Studios, the glorified garage just steps from Johnson's back door. And of course that the surf at Pipeline would be up.

Johnson had budgeted a rather long, by his standards, recording session of one month. But beyond that, the recording experience was conspicuous by its blueprint adherence to what had come before. Topol and Podlewski had quickly picked up on Johnson's new vibe and were able, through a leisurely rehearsal period, to find the perfect instrumental styles and shadings for each song. Zach Gill, who when not with Animal Liberation Orchestra had become a de facto member, both recording and touring, of Johnson's band, was on board to add piano and accordion which had naturally become an intregal part of the Jack Johnson sound.

'We just didn't want to have a plan,' said Johnson in an MTV interview. 'I just thought each record was going to get a little mellower. With this one, I think everyone was in a good mood in the studio so we ended up producing it a little bit more upbeat.'

Like its predecessor, *In Between Dreams* came together with lots of time out for surfing, hanging out and just basking in the island vibe. Children were very much a part of the scenery with sessions often stopping cold so that Johnson could spend some quality time with his wife and son. Caldato had, by this time, grown accustomed to the non-traditional approach to recording Johnson and his Brushfire labelmates and found himself forging new attitudes and production philosophies when recording at this non-chaotic rate.

Caldato knew at this juncture that Johnson literally had to do his own thing at his own pace. He was receptive to the producer's suggestions and would incorporate elements of mood and structure into his compositions. But easily the biggest thing that Caldato learned was that, in Jack Johnson's world, time was not money and that the album would be done when Johnson said it was done.

Johnson's own mindset to recording was to simply tune out the pressures associated with any expectations of *In Between Dreams* following up the massive commercial success of *On And On* and, in his words to simply 'goof off.'

Consequently, anyone expecting an unforeseen flash of brilliance on *In Between Dreams* were doomed to disappointment. It was once again Johnson and his musicians comfortably playing in Mango Tree Studios. While Johnson did concede that the sessions were marked by a sense of rawness and funk, the album, while not as glossy as its predecessors, still maintained the same kind of vibe.

But as the recording session progressed, it was becoming quite evident that, in his own subtle way, Johnson was pushing the envelope. The songs 'Better Together', a sincere rendering of the new love theme, and 'Banana Pancakes', a somewhat autobiographical tale of a rainy day spent inside, were vintage Johnson, long on sincerity and simplicity, thought and execution. If the rest of *In Between Dreams* had gone the familiar route, Johnson would have been ducking for cover and critics would have been having a field day. Because, in all honesty, this was very old news.

Fortunately Johnson on *In Between Dreams* was capable, even in the slightest moments, of mustering up a little fire in the belly. For all its softness, 'Sitting, Waiting, Wishing' is a sly jab at good riddance to a bad relationship. And no amount of lilting melody can disguise the fact that 'Good People' is taking shots at people who let television and the media influence their lives. Nothing on *In Between Dreams* draws blood but there is enough good natured jostling to indicate that Johnson had not gone completely soft.

Johnson was not sure which side of his musical vibe the album landed on.

'It's slightly more upbeat,' critiqued Johnson for MTV, 'but not very much. We weren't trying to put an edge on it but I do think that the album turned out to be a little less mellow than it turned out.'

True to his deal with Universal, when the album was locked down to his satisfaction, Johnson sent the tapes to the record company executives. Although they were contractually obligated to not change a note, they were quite happy with the finished product. Their bottom line was sales and that meant there had to be singles. And, to their way of thinking, at least a third of the cuts on the album were radio friendly.

By the time *In Between Dreams* was in the can, it was time to consider getting back on the road. True to his promise of keeping touring to a family-friendly minimum, the majority of dates fell into a four-week period from late-August to mid-September. The dates began with what Johnson considered a surreal experience with a show in the gambling mecca of Lake Tahoe California. The tour would follow the California coast for shows in Berkeley, Santa Barbara, Los Angeles and San Diego and was a chance to revisit the places that had supported Johnson before he struck it big. Then it would be on to the Midwest and finally to shows on the east coast.

The tour would be a triple bill of good friends with G. Love and Donovan Frankenreiter as the support acts. And with baby Moe now five months old and Kim up to the rigours of travel, it was decided that Johnson's family would accompany him on at least some of the dates.

Johnson was an old hand at the touring experience but having his wife and son along added a whole new element to life on the road for the singer. He would spend much of his non-concert time playing with Moe and enjoying watching as his son experienced things for the first time. The peace that Johnson had experienced on Oahu in the days following the birth of his son was recreated in a tour bus roaring across the United States.

'We take him on tour just about everywhere we go right now,' said Johnson, 'and he's so wide eyed about everything.'

The tour also offered the easy-going Kim a chance to see, for the first time in a long while, her husband as chick magnet. She would smile at the throngs of young women who would crowd the stage, laugh when they would bare their breasts in the face of their idol or throw their underwear at him and basically be the understanding and trusting wife.

'She's really cool about the whole thing,' he told *Chicago Innerview*. 'That's why I love her so much. We've been together 11 years now and she's seen the whole thing happen. Now, when there are girls around after the show, she just kind of laughs at the idea that there's anyone around that even wants to talk to me.'

The 2004 tour saw Jack Johnson at the height of his prowess as a performer. The nervousness that marked his early live performances was all but gone. The ease with which he handled the often-raucous atmosphere that would erupt in even the quietest musical moments was obvious. The shorthand between Topol and Podlewski was instinctive; each member knowing when it was time to give the other his moment in the spotlight before reverting back to a cohesive whole. The party atmosphere of the tour was helped by the presence of G. Love and Frankenreiter who would often make appearances in each other's sets and, before and after the shows, would often be found jamming together.

At one point on the tour, Johnson, Love and Frankenreiter invaded the studios of radio station KOS, a music and outdoor lifestyle show hosted by old friend Kelly Slater. It was almost to be expected that getting this group together would result in a musical interlude or two. But when these old friends got together, the memories and good feelings were at such a high level that it came as no surprise when a free wheeling all-star jam, that included Slater, erupted onto the airwaves. The songs were a mixture of each musician's library and included 'Rodeo Clowns', 'Free', 'Sunshine', 'Heading Home', and 'Mud Football'.

Frankenreiter had vivid memories of the impromptu jam session. 'It was just the three of us on acoustic guitars,' he related to *Transworld Surf*. 'It was just a really cool opportunity, having the time to just sit in the studio and jam. We all definitely have our kind of styles and I think they really lend themselves to each other.'

When the dust settled, Johnson saw the intrinsic value of this live jam and, after adding a strong rendition of 'Girl I Wanna Lay You Down' featuring Zach Gill from a Boston show, he decided to put a CD of the music out.

The year 2004 also saw a variety of Jack Johnson compositions make their way onto several compilation albums. His appearance at the Austin City Limits Music Festival in 2003 resulted in his rendition of the song 'Taylor' appearing on two mementos of that show, *Austin City Limits Music Festival 2003* and *2003 Collection: Live From Austin Texas*. A loose amalgamation of musical friends got together and the result was a one-shot album, credited to Handsome Boy Modeling School which contained a performance by Johnson of his song 'Breakdown'.

'One of Merlo's good friends is the producer Dan the Automator,' he related of his involvement in the Handsome Boy project to *Slap* magazine. 'When we first started coming through San Francisco, he would always come down and be at the shows. So I started meeting with him and we just stayed in touch. He contacted me about doing a track on the record and I was definitely up for it.'

During this period, Johnson also contributed his talents to a light-hearted album of children's orientated pop music called *Mary Had A Little Amp*, Johnson contributed the first recorded version of his ecology friendly song 'The 3 R's.

Although the tour had ended, Johnson managed to sneak in one more appearance before the end of the year and it was for a good cause. Johnson agreed to play the September 29 Vote For Change show in Phoenix, Arizona whose proceeds in this election year were to educate and mobilise in swing states. The intent was to defeat George Bush and the Republicans and Johnson, who shared the stage with Crosby, Stills & Nash, Jackson Browne, Bonnie Raitt and Keb Mo, was forthright in his support for the anti-Bush sentiments abroad in the land.

But it was the announcement that Johnson was appearing on the Vote For Change bill that would ultimately bring the first hint of a backlash against the singer and his politics.

'When I announced that I was going to do the show, there were people on my website's messageboard saying things like, "I like his music but I don't understand why he's suddenly talking about politics,"' recalled Johnson in a conversation with *The Independent*. 'Which is ridiculous, because I make lyrical music and if you don't want to hear my opinions you can't really listen to my songs. Fans on the site started a petition asking people to sign up if they didn't think I should play that show. It was weird because I was playing with people, any of who could have individually sold out the venue. But because we were performing under a political banner, we didn't even sell it out.'

Johnson had never worn his politics on his sleeve. To hear him describe it, he was neither a Republican or a Democrat. And while he admitted that he was living in a bubble whose friends all shared his opinions, he was particularly shocked that the reasonableness of an anti-Bush effort had not produced the desired result. It was the rare moment that Johnson admitted he might be out of touch with the rest of the world.

Might being the operative world. For while Johnson was not blind to what was going on outside his sedate life, the reality was that, for a good part of his life, he had shown little interest in anything outside of surfing and music. Johnson was coming to embrace causes relatively late and his naivety was definitely showing.

Nonetheless Johnson's US tour had been one of the high points, critically and financially, of the concert touring season. When it finished, he retired to Oahu at year's end to celebrate the holidays with his family and friends. His last official business act of 2004 had been to okay the release of his live jam, entitled *Some Live Songs* for an early December release.

As always Johnson was glad to be home and on the surf and was conscious of the thoughts of getting away from it all and back to his island paradise all the time. He would often acknowledge that even during a concert performance, his mind would occasionally blank out on the fact that he was performing in front of thousands of people and the only thing he could think of was being out on the waves with friends.

'I'll just think, "Man this is the last place I want to be right now,"' he acknowledged in *Launch*. 'You just feel like being away.'

Johnson saw in the New Year as a content and quite happy man. He was fulfilled as a husband and father. He was a guy who lived to surf and whose day job was as one of the biggest acts in popular music. What would come next was anybody's guess. And he was not laying awake nights thinking about it.

'The future,' he said to MTV, 'just kind of chooses me.'

10

Jack Is Curious George

Jack Johnson had been keeping a secret for a long time.

It was a fear born of a deep rooted insecurity and doubt that no amount of success had been able to shake. It was only with the imminent release of the album *In Between Dreams* that Johnson was able to admit that he had been insecure about the quality and strength of his songwriting and that his entire career to that point might have been nothing more than a big con on a gullible public.

It was an insecurity that had dogged the singer from the moment he had played his songs live. The discomfort only deepened with the release of *Brushfire Fairytales*, when the shock of writing songs that a lot of people connected with had sent him into an emotional tailspin. His true worth as a songwriter of substance had not changed with the even larger reception that greeted *On And On*.

'My sense that maybe it was all a fluke didn't really disappear until after that album (*In Between Dreams*),' he said in *Guitar World Acoustic*. 'I suddenly realised that I had put out three albums that listeners seemed to genuinely identify with.'

But while the strength of his songwriting was not in doubt, one long standing element of the Jack Johnson persona had never been put to the test. Could he simply be a writer for hire? Johnson had long been an admirer of songwriters and had a particular affinity for such legendary Tin Pan Alley legends as Irving Berlin, Carol King, Burt Bacharach and the legendary team of Leiber and Stoller and he believed that his soundtracks for the surf movies *Thicker Than Water* and *The September Sessions* were essentially that kind of work.

But it had been a work that was, at its core, near and dear to him emotionally and spiritually. He drew satisfaction from his ability to craft music that complimented the images he had created for the screen.

However since his rise in popularity, Johnson had received numerous offers to create original music for movie and television soundtracks and had declined them all on the grounds that he could not simply write a song to order and that his independent nature would not allow others to have a say in his creative process.

But Johnson would be the first to admit that his mind was in a different place during the recording of *In Between Dreams*, when his manager contacted him with an offer to do some songs for the animated film version of the time-honoured children's book, *Curious George*. He had grown up with the *Curious George* books and, although not a true fan, he had always been enamoured of the image and the messages of the books.

Even more important, with the recent birth of his son, Johnson was feeling a real connection to his inner child and felt it would be fun to write songs that would contain the energy of youth. So it was a surprise to those around him when Johnson threw his hat into the ring.

It was not a decision totally supported by the more media savvy critics who happened upon the story early on. Many, perhaps feeling that Johnson still only had a fragile grip on a career, suggested that he would be better served by going into the studio and producing another album of his patented laidback island songs rather than risking his reputation by trying to reach a target audience that topped out at age ten. Still others acknowledged that Johnson had had a free ride, creatively, to this point and that suddenly being thrust into an arena of creativity by committee could well do some damage to what they felt was the singer's fragile ego.

Johnson would later acknowledge that much of those same thoughts had been on his mind and, while couching it in laughs, conceded that doing a kids album could well end his career.

But ever the pragmatist, he would logically make a case for his being able to write for a younger audience.

'I'm a pretty simple guy and I think kids already relate a lot to the songs,' he explained to *Ninemsn*. 'I don't know if that's a compliment or a dis but I get that a lot. There are songs where I just try to tap into those (childlike) feelings of bliss and hitting your stride and when everything seems perfect. And those are my favorite songs, the ones that feel like that. I've been trying to write more of those and so this is a perfect time to do a kid's record.'

The singer would later discover that he was actually on a shortlist of respected composers who had been contacted about the *Curious George* project. But Johnson's barely contained enthusiasm for what would be his first 'big time' music job and his willingness to put aside his feelings about writing music for an already-completed film, ultimately landed him the assignment.

Still, the songwriter remained cautious. The film's producers sensed this and so decided to slowly ease Johnson into the work. They initially asked if he would write just one song for the film and Johnson readily agreed. Johnson soon received a couple of brief segments for a pair of scenes from the film to use as a guide to capturing the particular emotion of that element of the film. His creative tank still quite full in the wake of *In Between Dreams*, Johnson immediately set to work.

Harkening back to the days of scoring his surf films, Johnson retired to his studio where he played the segments over and over. A vibe soon settled in and Johnson began inputting some ideas on to a four-track tape. Johnson eventually came up with what he felt was a nice, kid-friendly, upbeat tune called 'Talk Of The Town'. As with most Johnson compositions, the inspiration behind 'Talk Of The Town' was a fairly simple one. The singer had been sitting out on the shore one day, watching the sunset. The next day some friends of his were talking to Johnson about what a beautiful sunset it had been. Johnson was quite amused that such a big deal had been made out of such a natural thing and the lyrics were soon flowing.

Johnson completed the song and shipped it off to the producers who were knocked out by what they heard. They continued the casual courtship of Johnson by asking if he could possibly come up with a second song to go with the segments they were sending him.

By now, quietly pleased with himself, Johnson readily agreed.

The second assignment was a different sort of challenge. For a sequence in which Curious George had to deal with being separated from the Man In The Yellow Hat, Johnson had to emotionally switch gears. Unlike the first song, which musically and thematically was not too far removed from Johnson's strength as a songwriter, the song that would become the melancholy 'Wrong Turn' gave the composer an insight into how film music can have a powerful impact on the story being told. Johnson reached down deep inside and found the sadness that only a child could feel. After turning in 'Wrong Turn', Johnson was hooked.

'I don't know if it was their intention to slowly get me to do the whole thing,' recalled Johnson in *Guitar World Acoustic,*' but I kind of beat them to the punch by saying, "If there's more, I'm excited to do as much as you guys want."'

Johnson would not be under any extreme deadlines on his *Curious George* score as the movie was not scheduled to be released until early 2006 and would allow him the leisurely creative time he craved as well as giving him time to deal with the last minute details of the March 1, 2005 release of *In Between Dreams.*

One of the most hilarious elements of marketing the new album was the inevitable video for the album's first single, 'Sitting, Waiting, Wishing'. In it, Johnson would be required to recite the words to the song backwards. Johnson made every attempt to study his own lyrics prior to the shoot but his memory failed him at the last possible moment when, with his headphones on, he threw up his hands in disgust and said he could not do it. Thanks to some strategically placed cue cards, Johnson was finally able to sing his own song backwards but he often jokes that the lip-synching is way off in certain parts of the video.

It had become almost routine for Jack Johnson's albums to jump out of the starting blocks and up the charts. But Johnson never imagined that *In Between Dreams* would better his previous album's debut and open at number two on the national charts. The album's reception was not surprising. Radio stations were all over the first single, 'Sitting, Waiting, Wishing' and the fans raced to purchase their copy. Years of cultivating a sincere relationship with his audience over the years had succeeded in planting the seeds of a very large and very loyal following.

Also not surprising was the critical reception the album received. The trade press (who never met an album they could not find something good to say about) and the fan-oriented websites were almost universal in their praise for the album; some quite insightfully focusing on the harder-edged social commentary that had seeped into some of the songs. And finally, it was a given that the mainstream pop culture press would continue to bash Johnson at every turn.

Rolling Stone came the closest it had ever come to a rave in its review of *In Between Dreams* but still could not resist the sly shot when it offered 'Johnson seems to think that his smooth acoustic surfer image might need a retooling to reflect this scary new world. On "Crying Shame" and "Staple It Together", he attacks warmongering and the chronically denial-ridden.'

Entertainment Weekly chimed in with 'He is so laidback it is hard to tell when he's worked up. In more encouraging news, his songs are meatier.'

Blender dropped this bomb: 'An assured yet unsatisfying shamble.'

Prefix magazine was no less critical: 'After nearly half a decade, Johnson still hasn't learned anything about time signatures and experimentation.'

And finally the always fence-sitting *Q* magazine offered up this back-handed compliment: 'It's his best work to date because at least he actually sounds awake.'

Johnson had always been selective in reading his critical notices and, by this time, was amused at how the critical barbs always seemed to revolve around his laidback image. It was as if the quality of the music was almost an afterthought. Johnson, in the weeks to come, would often defend his musical intent on *In Between Dreams*.

'I was trying to write a record that was mostly love songs or family songs,' he explained to MTV. 'They were songs about losing people you love and gaining people you love, songs about birth and death. That's what I was aiming for.'

He also offered up a spirited defense to the charges that all of his music basically sounded the same.

'I think the responsibility is to stick to your game,' he told an AP Radio interviewer. 'If you were just making people dance before and suddenly you become popular, I don't think you should change everything you do and start talking about politics. You should keep making people dance.'

But in the same breath, he told AP Radio that a closer look at his albums would show that he does mix things up a little.

'I have songs like "Bubble Toes" and then I have songs like "Crying Shame" that talk about the war in Iraq. I mostly just go off feel.'

Flushed with the success of *In Between Dreams* and the idea that he could successfully, at least so far, navigate the corporate side of music making with *Curious George*, Johnson became involved in a series of off-beat side projects.

He had long-counted West Coast punk band Sublime as a powerful influence on his music and was thrilled when he was asked to contribute a Sublime cover song to the tribute album *Look At The Love We Found: A Tribute To Sublime*. Johnson chose to do a progressive medley of his two favourite Sublime tracks, 'Bad Fish' and 'Boss DJ.'

For a light-hearted Christmas compilation entitled *A Winter's Night*, he resurrected his 2002 rendition of 'Rudolph The Red-Nosed Reindeer'. And finally, his involvement and friendship with Animal Liberation Orchestra resulted in his contributing his song 'Fly Between Falls' to their latest album.

Johnson treasured what many musicians would consider these 'throwaway' vanity projects. They allowed him to be more relaxed (as if such a thing was possible), hang with good friends and fellow musicians and to let his hair down in a non-pressure atmosphere.

With the release of *In Between Dreams*, Johnson grudgingly embarked on his least favourite element of being a music man, the almost non-stop press and promotion that accompanied a major new album. In many cases, it required him to appear in record stores, occasionally play a song or two and to smile and make good-natured small talk while signing an endless number of CDs. Despite the pressure of his fame and what he termed 'the craziness' of touring and promotion, Johnson would often acknowledge during this period in his life that he was fairly comfortable in his skin.

'I feel good where I'm at right now,' Johnson said in an interview with MTV shortly before an appearance at a Los Angeles record store. 'I don't get recognised when I'm on the streets but we're still able to draw a crowd and play a show. That's sort of the perfect balance for me.'

However Johnson did not have a lot of time to consider his place in the universe. Because what Johnson was finding as he delved deeper into creating music for *Curious George* was that it was often a time-consuming, often tedious process made all the more so by virtue of the fact that everything had to be run by a committee that included the film's producers, director and, ultimately, the movie studio releasing the film. This was the classic showdown between art and commerce that Johnson would later admit was so alien to his normal way of making music that he was uncomfortable with it at first. But his excitement eventually overrode his fear of having to compromise.

The process for Johnson creating further songs for *Curious George* began with the songwriter receiving the screenplay for the movie so that he could get a grasp of the storyline and how his music would fit in. This was followed by a series of sketches from the filmmakers and explanations of the scenes they wanted songs for. Johnson would respond with a rough sketch of a song. The filmmakers would, in turn, animate the sequence to fit the song. Johnson would receive notes on how long they felt the song should be. They would also show the songwriter more detailed photos and he would respond with more detailed lyrics.

'It wasn't like I would just finish a song and give it to them,' recalled Johnson in *Glide* magazine. 'A lot of times they'd send it back with notes. There'd be situations where they would want to move it around a little, when certain lyrics would just fit really well with something going on at a different time in the film. There was a lot of rearranging of the songs.'

Besides writing his own material, Johnson was given carte blanche to incorporate songs from other artists and, in this area, his business as well as personal sense came into play as he immediately opened the door to his label mates for additional material. 'The Sharing Song' was written by his drummer Adam Topol and piano-player and Animal Liberation Orchestra member Zach Gill. 'Lullaby' was written by surfing buddy and recent addition to the Brushfire roster Matt Costa. Johnson did duets with G. Love (on the G. Love song 'Jungle Gym') and Matt Costa on a couple of songs, and covered The White Stripes' 'We're Going To Be Friends.' He also managed to make his ecology-friendly kids' number 'The 3 R's' fit into *Curious George*'s world. Of course it would not have been a Jack Johnson project without a contribution from his dear friend Ben Harper.

'I got a call from Jack saying "I'm doing this thing, I'm going to send you some footage and some of the musical direction that I've got going so far and see if you've got anything for it," related Harper in a *Glide* magazine article. 'He'd mentioned that a stripped-down version of "My Own Two Hands" might be cool so he sent me the gear and I immediately locked onto where he was taking it musically. I laid down a version of "Two Hands", sent it over to him and he flossed on it as well. I was very excited to get that back and to see how it came out.'

As work on the soundtrack progressed, Johnson found himself faced with a couple of challenges. The first being that the character of Curious George never speaks. This entailed much trial and error as Johnson would spend long hours attempting to connect with the emotions of the character and then convey them in a song. The second was how to plug into the emotions and feelings of the film's target audience while creating in the relative solitude and sterility of his recording studio. Johnson solved that problem by literally opening his studio door to every kid on the island of Oahu.

'My kid was in the studio the whole time,' he recalled in *Guitar World Acoustic*. 'Not just him, but also my brother's kids and all their friends. We told everybody, "Bring as many of them as you can." The last thing I wanted to do was to sit in there (the studio) slaving over some record that wouldn't even connect with children. So the kids were there all the time, listening and dancing in the control room.'

When not recording, Johnson was gearing up for his first concert appearances of the year. The 2005 slate began on March 17 with a series of shows in Australia. In April, he headlined the annual Kokua Festival with Jackson Browne, Ozomatli and G. Love & Special Sauce. Two more stateside festivals, The New Orleans Jazz and Heritage Festival and the Beale Street Music Festival in Memphis, Tennessee, closed out April. This was followed by another jaunt across the pond in May for stops in New Zealand and Japan. Johnson returned to the States in early June to perform at the fifth annual Bonnaroo Festival which featured Dave Matthews, Jurassic 5, Modest Mouse and The Black Crowes.

Although his performance was often dwarfed in these massive outdoor settings by less-than-perfect sound systems and poor visibility, Johnson would maintain he had a soft spot in his heart for the big outdoor shows.

'I love those camping style festivals where you kind of get into a zone,' he explained. 'Because sometimes it goes by so quick, you're on your way home and you're just getting that feeling going.'

When contemplating touring, Johnson's thoughts always went to how his shows might benefit others in a charitable and ecological way. His 2005 tour of the states, which ran from August to mid-September, would be no different.

The destruction caused in New Orleans by Hurricane Katrina had resonated deeply with Johnson. Through the Red Cross, the singer established several fundraisers designed to help homeless and struggling

Katrina victims. Johnson also allotted $5,000 from every show between August 31 and September 13 (13 shows in all) for Katrina relief. In all, Johnson managed to raise more than $123,000 for hurricane relief.

On the ecology front, Johnson continued to push his eco-friendly tour as a teaching tool for the younger generation that turned to him for guidance. While continuing to rely on biodegradable diesel fuel to power his tour buses, Johnson continued to expand upon the ways he could take his world-friendly message directly to the fans.

Fans were encouraged to purchase reusable water bottles and Hemp tote bags to cut down on waste. Even the merchandise being sold on his tour was an eco-friendly alternative. Jack Johnson posters were printed on recyclable paper while T-shirts were made of organic cotton. And when it came to his concert rider, Johnson easily had the most unusual. Each venue where he played was required to have at least two dozen recycling sites and low-energy light bulbs on the concert grounds. He also insisted that bathroom facilities contain recyclable trash bags, paper towels and toilet paper.

'We tried to integrate as many of Jack's suggestions as possible,' concert promoter Seth Hurwitz told *Treehugger.com*. 'Coming from someone like Jack Johnson, who takes these matters to heart, makes it that much more meaningful. We plan to incorporate some of the changes into our standard operations. We will always think of Jack as the guy who inspired us to take that step.'

Admittedly this was a daunting task for concert promoters used to the usual concert riders of certain foods and designer waters. And more than one promoter revealed that it was not easy to comply with Johnson's ecology-friendly edict. But comply they did. Because Jack Johnson said so.

'I started to look at where we were going and I wanted to do something that could make a little less of an ecological footprint,' he offered MTV. 'Now that I'm in a position where I can do good, I've personally felt the responsibility to put the light on some issues that are bigger than myself.'

Combining pop music and ecology in a way that dwarfed even his earlier efforts, Johnson acknowledged that it was all one big learning process that had its share of bumps in the road. He admitted that the on-site recycling programme was hit or miss as some concert venues were just not set up for the process. He points to the distribution of any leftover backstage food to local shelters as a major success. And his ego was tweaked mildly when the cable news outlet CNN came on the road to report on Johnson's ecological side.

'I thought, if nothing else, it brought some attention to the idea that you can change things instead of just falling into the pattern of what people had previously done in any profession,' he assessed in the *Honolulu Advertiser*. 'In my case, it's touring. You can actually try something different and there are options.'

The US portion of the tour had been a particularly enjoyable time. Once again, Kim and Moe had accompanied Johnson which helped keep him in a relaxed state of mind. And Johnson had generously opened up the support slots on the tour to Animal Liberation Orchestra and Matt Costa. That they were friends made the tour easier on all counts but it also highlighted a sure business sense on Johnson's part by allowing acts, whose success would ultimately benefit Brushfire and himself, the major exposure and increased album sales that inevitably accompanied a long, high profile tour.

Throughout the remainder of 2005, Johnson continued in a beehive of activity. When he was not touring, he would be back at Oahu, attempting to catch his breath while finishing up the *Curious George* soundtrack. He also oversaw the release of the soundtrack of the film *Sprout*, which showcased Johnson in his favourite behind-the-scenes capacity as just a member of the band. Johnson was enjoying being at the centre of so much creative activity but he was also beginning to tire of it as well.

He had cut back on press interviews for the most part and those few that he did would eventually get around to his speculating on his immediate future. He would hint that he might like to take some time off and just disappear and do another surf film. He also indicated that, with the *Curious George* soundtrack now on his resumé, he might concentrate on projects that would not require him to be in the spotlight. Of course spending time with his wife and child remained his number one priority. While never admitting to complete exhaustion, Johnson, on more than one occasion, did indicate that he might take 2006 off and do absolutely nothing.

Those around Johnson had heard the refrain before and, as in the past, it would be the bean counters and suits who would warn the singer that pop music is fickle and that a year away from the public might find his fans turning in another direction. Johnson was not concerned.

He has never been the type to worry about whether his fans might one day desert him. His fall-back position being that he never expected to get as far with his music as he had and did not think it would be a big deal if he did take a break and came back at a later date. He was finally secure in the fact that whether or not his fans came back was, quite simply, no big deal.

Johnson was in a perfect place to feel confident in any future career decisions. *In Between Dreams* had, while once again failing to hit number one on the U.S. album charts, sold in excess of two million copies in record time. The album would, in fact, reach the top spot on the British charts; leaving no doubt of Johnson's worldwide appeal and confirming a growing fan base that would surely survive his packing it all in for a while.

If Johnson were to go on an extended break, he was going to leave his fans with one last nugget. Midway through 2005, the idea was floated to release a 2 DVD set entitled *A Weekend At The Greek* by Jack Johnson and Friends.

The set would contain two complete live shows of Johnson in concert in 2005 at The Greek in Berkeley, California and a show recorded in Japan from the 2004 *On And On* tour. Edited together in documentary-cinema verité style, *A Weekend At The Greek* would be a literal documentary of life on the road with backstage interviews, informal moments and interviews with Johnson and the members of his band, entourage, and the heavy friends who supported him on those shows.

The genesis of the idea came in 2004 when Johnson decided to shoot some footage of the tour. Johnson was not sure if the material would actually be used or just end up on a shelf but thought the idea of getting what he considered 'the fun culture' of Japan would be worth the effort. The approach to shooting the Japan footage was real low budget and very retro. For the concert footage filmed at shows in Osaka, Tokyo and Fuji and the shots of Johnson and friends surfing or just goofing off, the crew used 60s and 70s Bolex-style cameras that played havoc with the sound and the final result was often the equivalent of a badly-dubbed foreign film.

Johnson's business acumen was once again brought to the fore with the release of the DVD. The singer, well-advised by his managers and record label, realised that the DVD package was a good dollars and cents move, guaranteed to make money. But Johnson insisted that nothing would go out under his name that did not have some intrinsic creative and artistic merit to it. And taken as a strictly cinematic effort, the documentary style package does indeed hold up for both loyal fans and those new on the Jack Johnson scene.

By the time Johnson began touring behind the *On And On* album, the project began taking on a bit more steam and the result is a more detailed look into the lives of Johnson and his musician friends as they toured the States.

Johnson liked the idea of a concert package done up much the way his surf movies had been: devoid of pretence and with a quite natural sense of time and space. And needless to say, Universal, who released *A Weekend At The Greek* on November 20, 2005, was quite happy to have something available for the Christmas shopping season. Further evidence of Johnson's superstar status came when the DVD was certified double platinum in a matter of months.

Once again Johnson was at home for the holidays. By now his routine had become rote; the perfect balance of minimal touring and leisurely re-cording that had produced songs that had enraptured millions. Johnson had it all but he remained cautiously optimistic about his pop star world getting any bigger.

His mantra remained quite simple. Continue a low key career of put-ting out records without a whole lot of hype and sell enough records to at least break even. Most would look at Johnson's pronouncements at a point where his albums were going platinum and he was selling out major venues as a bit pretentious. But Johnson remained nothing if not totally sincere in the modest goals he had set for himself and had achieved.

'I've tried to realise what it is and to not get sucked into overthinking music and treating it as too important,' he said in an *Associated Press* in-terview. 'It's still kind of just feel-good music that's fun to make.'

He would tell anyone who would listen that all the choices that he was making in his career were based on how much fun they were bringing into his life and those of his family and friends. He pointed out that he was quite comfortable with the way things were at this point and was not making any plans to change anything.

'I really don't want things to get any bigger than they already are,' he offered in a London *Evening Standard* profile. 'The film (*Curious George*) is a step in the right direction for me. It's moving me more towards the background.'

As with the perks of stardom, Johnson was also being bombarded with the temptations. The offers of longer and longer tours in larger and larger venues had come with more consistency. There was also the not-too-veiled suggestions that it would be great if Johnson could squeeze out an album a year. On the up side, there was the beginning of a trickle of offers for Johnson to do more soundtrack work. The former two enticements he dismissed out of hand. The latter he gave serious consideration to.

But to Johnson's way of thinking, even that phase of his career was going to have to wait.

'We definitely haven't bought any Porsches or anything like that,' Johnson told *Chicago Innerview* in response to a question regarding keeping up his lifestyle. 'I still just drive a soccer mom minivan. We've maintained a pretty easy life to afford. Eventually I want to be able to slow down and not tour so much while my kids are in school. That's what everyone wishes but I think I can achieve it.'

Kim would often echo Johnson's statements about keeping their lifestyle at a simple, manageable level. 'I don't want people to think that we're line drying all our clothes or generating all our own electricity,' she laughingly told the *Honolulu Weekly*. 'We'd love to and maybe we'll get there someday. But our lives are about other things right now. We just try to do the best we can.'

Johnson's passion was now finally front and centre on his to-do-list as he applied the brakes to his career.

'We're probably going to take a solid year or two off,' he reported to MTV News. 'I'm ready to catch up on surfing.'

11

The News Today

Jack Johnson did not pay too much attention to the music industry. He rarely watched MTV (or much TV at all) to see what was new and hip on the scene. He did not read *Billboard* except to occasionally take a peek at the charts. Jack Johnson took it as a definite plus to his individuality that he was in the music business but could quite effectively operate outside its grasp.

When it came to business, Jack Johnson may have played dumb but he was nobody's fool. He would regularly meet with and / or talk to Emmet Malloy to discuss the dollars and cents side of things and what had to be addressed immediately and what could wait. That Malloy and Johnson had developed a short hand over the years made the whole process easier for Johnson to digest.

It was enough for him to know that there was a great, complex, black hole of a process that made it possible for him to create music, for the people to like it and that, somehow, the business side allowed him to make a living doing what he loved to do. But Johnson was not naïve. He knew enough about how the music industry worked to realise that the rewards would never come to him in the form of a little gold statue.

So despite the fact that the prestigious Grammy Awards, as recently as 2003, had taken a definite swing back in the direction of the singer-song-writer over glitz and rock pomposity, Johnson was all but ignoring his chances as the hype surrounding the 2006 Grammys began to play out.

'I guess if that's going to mean that things are going to move in that direction, it really doesn't matter too much,' he reflected in a *Launch* magazine article. 'Sometimes I think the music I play almost doesn't get too popular and become mainstream because I tend to like stuff that's just below the real mainstream. I'm somewhat part of the counter culture and I don't mind being a part of that.'

Johnson's response may well have been a subconscious defence mechanism against the inevitable disappointment that he felt would most surely come. From the release of *Brushfire Fairytales* onwards, there had been whispers and slight groundswells of support for Johnson picking up a nomination or two. But in the eyes of those in the industry who made those kinds of decisions, Johnson had been considered too slight, too inconsequential and, finally, in the unkindest of backhanded compliments, too unimportant to be considered for high honours.

Whether Johnson took those slights to heart is open to conjecture. Sour grapes not being a part of Johnson's makeup, it has rarely, if ever, been noted that the singer harboured the slightest resentment of the snubs.

However into 2006, that was all about to change. The first to recognise Johnson's worth and contributions to popular music were the British who knocked Johnson over with a literal feather when they announced that the mild-mannered Yank had been nominated in two categories for the prestigious 2006 Brit Awards, for Best International Male Artist and International Breakthrough Artist.

Johnson had become a real fan favourite across the pond and his albums, despite the British propensity for larger-than-life angst-ridden and overly-theatrical performers, had done fairly well in England. In his own quiet way, Johnson was grateful for the recognition even though he felt it was a given that he would not win on awards night.

The unexpected recognition continued when the Grammy nominations came out and Johnson was nominated for Best Pop Vocalist in a group that included Paul McCartney, Stevie Wonder and Seal, and for Best Pop Song Collaboration with vocals for his work on the long-delayed Black Eyed Peas song 'Gone Going'. When he heard the news, Johnson thought it was a joke. For how could they nominate somebody for a singing award when, in Johnson's own estimation, they could not sing.

'I feel that I'm totally out of my league,' he said in response to the nominations in a *Contactmusic.com* news item. 'The Best Pop Vocal is a category I would never expect to be put in. I have confidence in writing songs but if you're going off in vocal, let's give it to Stevie Wonder or Seal right off the bat. I've always written songs with a lot of syllables so I don't have to hold onto a note. I don't think I can ever sing in key. It's cool but it's weird. It's something I never experienced at all. I just hope I get to hang out backstage.'

Johnson was prophetic in his statement. He did go to the Grammys and did get to hang out backstage and meet some of his heroes. And when he lost Best Pop Vocal to Stevie Wonder, he was not surprised and all the better for the experience.

'I was actually pretty stoked that Stevie Wonder won,' he recalled in the *Honolulu Advertiser*. 'I was thinking, it's pretty cool to say you were nominated the same year that Stevie Wonder got it. He's about as cool a human as I can think of to lose to.'

The singer laughingly recalled in a *Honolulu Advertiser* interview that it was a weird scene and that he felt totally out of his element.

'I had a suit on and the whole deal. But it was fun. I had a hunch that I wasn't going to win so I wasn't that nervous about having to go up and give a speech or anything. I was more nervous just to be in a suit.'

Around the time of the Grammy announcement, the first defection from the idyllic world of Jack Johnson came when his long time friend Donovan Frankenreiter announced that he would be leaving Brushfire Records and would be releasing his latest album, *Move By Yourself*, on the Lost Highway label. Rumours were immediately rampant that Frankenreiter and Johnson had had an unpleasant falling out and that Johnson's reportedly quiet, dictatorial ways had driven Frankenreiter to leave.

The more tabloid elements of the press were suddenly chomping at the bit. They apparently loved the notion that the nicest guy in the world actually had an ego-driven dark side. As it turned out, the feeding frenzy was finished before it started.

Frankenreiter, during a recent Australian tour, was quick to point out that the two musicians remained close friends. He further revealed, not too surprisingly, that his departure was due to creative differences; due in large part to the fact that despite having a slightly funkier, soulful sound than Johnson's, he was constantly being lumped in with Johnson's softer, island sound.

'It was kind of hard for me to break away and be myself, be my own artist, my own musician,' declared Frankenreiter in a *Sunday Mail* interview. 'Everything I did always got entwined and combined with me trying to be another Jack Johnson. I never wanted to be that and it was one of those things I thought I would never be able to break away from. Jack totally understood. He wants the best for me and he said this will never get in the way of our friendship.'

Inevitably Johnson was beginning to hear the 'sell out' tag from pockets of supporters who knew him when nobody else did and now found it hard to accept the idea that Johnson was a fan-favourite of millions. The attacks were, for the most part, empty or vague; claiming that Johnson had deliberately changed his style of music to cater to mainstream tastes. Johnson never thought enough of the attacks to comment on them, although he did stick to his personal mantra of just putting the music out there and leaving it up to people whether they liked it or not.

While Johnson was attempting to find comfort in this strange new spotlight, the wheels of the business around him ground steadily forward. The *Curious George* soundtrack, now titled *Sing-A-Longs And Lullabies For The Film Curious George*, was scheduled for a February 7 release. Johnson had been looking forward to the album coming out for a number of reasons. It had been a true test of his talents in a more structured atmosphere. It was something he felt was a valid distillation of his feelings about fatherhood and family. But the true creative spirit in him was proud of his having made a children's album that was not just for kids.

The singer-songwriter has been the first to acknowledge that it would not have taken much talent to merely slog out a series of cute and cuddly songs aimed solely at the very young. But Johnson felt he had taken that all important next step, creatively, and crafted songs that, musically and lyrically, had as much appeal to adults as they did to children. In Johnson's eyes, he had made a real record.

As he awaited the start of his work year, Johnson was continuing to savour each moment on his island paradise. He was making every effort to spend at least two hours a day surfing. It was literally the only time of the day that Johnson could be truly alone. Sometimes this solitude would result in a lyric or a song idea. But mostly he stated that his time on the water was his time to tune out of the business world.

He insisted during those times that he would be in a literal meditative vacuum. Nobody could ask him a question he would have to answer and the solitude of the ocean gave him ample opportunity to reflect on his life and where he was going.

Sing-A-Longs And Lullabies For The Film Curious George was released on February 7, 2006 and while Johnson was hoping that it would be successful, he could not have been prepared for the massive response to the album. The soundtrack sold an immediate 162,000 copies and debuted at number one on the national album charts. The first single off the album, 'Upside Down', was an instant add on most major radio playlists.

Sing-A-Longs And Lullabies For The Film Curious George was also the rare album that would end up having more life than the movie that spawned it. For despite the filmmaker's best efforts, *Curious George* received only mixed reviews and was only moderately successful in reaching its target audience. Consequently the movie was quickly sliding to smaller screens and fewer theatres while the album was just beginning to take off.

Johnson was both pleased and relieved that adults had responded to the album with the same enthusiasm as children. However, given his history with critics, he was not holding his breath for a sudden rush of good reviews. And to their credit, the critics did not disappoint. While most acknowledged that the album was light years above the banal offerings of most children's movie soundtracks, they were quick to point out that it was still Jack Johnson doing what he did best, which to their way of thinking, was the same old thing.

Rolling Stone weighed in with their usual smart alec assessment: 'Not one to strain himself, but underrated in his own polite way, Jack Johnson keeps his regular dude croon friendly and extra bright on this quietly pretty soundtrack.'

Jambands.com offered: 'While kids may catch the vibe that is Johnson's musical aesthetic, it is truly the children lurking within the elders who will find the most satisfaction in *Curious George*.'

Entertainment Weekly assessed the album this way: 'It's a set of breezy, sun-baked folk-pop that's not unlike a typical Johnson album.'

Johnson was particularly amused by the fact that his arch nemesis *Rolling Stone* had finally given him, by their standards, a good review.

'They love me now,' he laughed during a *Honolulu Advertiser* interview. 'They finally gave me three stars.'

Although widely perceived as a distinctly American artist, Johnson was now finding that his overseas image was beginning to change. In most countries, typified by his early 2006 concert appearances in New Zealand

and Japan, Johnson had been welcomed and embraced with all the enthusiasm accorded the latest pop flavour of the moment.

But while equally popular in England, Johnson was seen as something a bit more mythic and substantial. From the outset, Johnson had been treated by the press as more of a curiosity who had seemingly stumbled into their midst from another planet and whose style of music, while endearing, was a bit of a mystery. But as he prepared to go to England for a late February-early March tour, Johnson sensed a difference in the way he was being dealt with across the pond.

There was the Brit Award nominations to consider and at a time when the British pop music scene was seemingly more flash and trash than substance, Johnson's inclusion was considered a surprise concession of simplicity. But also there was the sudden and massive pre-sale of tickets to Johnson's shows that had caused such a stir that some dates had to be moved to larger venues and additional nights were added.

Johnson's reaction was to smile, give thanks to his British fans and, as always to quietly marvel at his continued good fortune. As he hopped a plane for the other side of the pond, he did not know what to expect.

When Johnson landed in England, he was astonished to find billboards proclaiming him the new Dylan everywhere he went. The Brit Awards were an amusing counter to the staid Grammys. For openers, he did not have to wear a suit. Wine was served to the assembled audience during the course of the show which, to Johnson's observation, resulted 'in a lot more funny stuff' when it came time for acceptance speeches.

Johnson celebrated his winning the International Breakthrough Artist honours by holding an audience of thousands spellbound as he sat stage centre on a stool with his trusty acoustic, plucking and singing softly the song 'Better Together'.

'Kanye West was the performer before me and he had 70 girls in bathing suits all painted gold,' chuckled Johnson in a *Honolulu Advertiser* interview. 'The Gorillaz played after me and they had about a hundred elementary school kids up there singing with them. And in between I came out with just an acoustic guitar. I ended up standing out. It was pretty funny. It was cool. It was a good time.'

Rather than dealing with Johnson as just another flavour of the moment, the notoriously cranky British press was now intent on delving deep into the Johnson mystique, asking probing questions and treating the shy performer with the respect usually reserved for somebody who they feel will be around for a while.

While his history was once more explored to the point where Johnson could almost recite the high points in his sleep, he was encouraged by the British perspective on his very American story and anxious to expound on issues that were important to him and that had worldwide implications. The foreign press seemed particularly anxious to explore his ecological attitudes and social agendas and Johnson was only too happy to reply.

Easily the highlight of the British tour was the headlining show at the famed London Hammersmith Apollo. As one critic summed up the appearance, 'Jack Johnson could scratch his ass, pick his nose and eat it and still provoke shrills of delight.' But there was more to that show than mere mania.

Despite the size of the hall, Johnson, from song one, was able to move the audience on the strength of warm feelings, a mellow island vibe and, of course, good songs. Johnson was definitely into giving the British their money's worth as he played a generous selection from all three of his albums before kicking into playful gear at the encore with Sublime and Pearl Jam covers before leaving the audience with a peaceful easy feeling with a heartfelt rendition of 'Better Together'.

Johnson was very much a kid at play during this latest European trek. The tour caught Switzerland in the dead of winter. But the singer was not adverse to snowboarding on the Swiss Alps when he could not catch a wave. Snow was not a problem in Portugal where Johnson took this patch of warm weather as an excuse to hit the beach.

Johnson returned to the states and a few weeks of laying out in the sun and doing some light housekeeping around his backyard when some slight landfalls off the nearby mountains caused huge ruts in the road. Seeing Johnson shirtless, bending his back with shovel in hand told a lot about how Johnson had maintained his humanity. He could have easily hired somebody to do the heavy work but he thought nothing about doing it himself.

It was not long before Johnson began preparing for the second phase of the 2006 touring season which began April 19 with the third annual Kokua Festival. This year's line-up featured a number of local Hawaiian musicians as well as old friend Ben Harper and the inclusion of cause-friendly outlaw country legend Willie Nelson. Johnson was like a kid in a candy shop as he happily hung out backstage with his musical heroes, was primed to play a joyous set for the thousands in attendance and was at ease with the idea that he was using his talents for the benefit of the planet.

With his long standing relationship with Animal Liberation Orchestra, it was just a matter of ringing up some friends and asking them to come and play. A chance encounter at a kickball tournament performance resulted in an invitation to Paula Fuga and an ongoing phone relationship landed Henry Kapono. But the real prize for Kokua III was the ability to get the elusive Ben Harper to commit.

'It finally just worked out on his schedule,' recalled Johnson in a *Rolling Stone* article. 'He actually almost came the first year. I talked to him at the last minute then and he was thinking about just coming over and doing a surprise guest thing. The second year it just didn't work out with his schedule. This year we asked him far enough in advance that he went ahead and said, "You know what, I'm just gonna commit to it and then work my schedule around it."'

Assembling the line-up for Kokua III was a fairly easy process due, in large part, to Johnson's celebrity status and his ability to make friends with just about anybody. The singer had met Willie Nelson the previous year and had gotten along famously which led to Johnson asking and Nelson immediately accepting an invitation to play at the concert.

Kokua Festival III was a mixture of styles and sensibilities. The Animal Liberation Orchestra opened things up with a tasty set of laidback funk while local artists Henry Kapono and Paula Fuga added strains of traditional island sounds and reggae into the mix. Ben Harper was in a totally mellow mood, playing simple acoustic guitar while avoiding his more aggressive message songs and Willie Nelson had the crowd on their feet with a mixture of his greatest hits and new country songs.

All of which led up to Johnson's headlining set. The singer was in a relaxed mood and it showed in a loosely structured version of Bob Marley's 'Stir It Up' and an upbeat version of the melancholy 'Good People'. A sparkling rendition of Kenny Loggin's 'Danny's Song' led into an all-star finale as Harper joined Johnson on stage for 'Flake' and 'Two Hands' and Nelson made it a trio on the song 'Blue Eyes'. The set was typical of the power Johnson had come to wield onstage. The power to make people feel good.

Johnson broke new ground in April with his first tour of Brazil. In a handful of shows, his quiet demeanour easily won over a Brazilian audience that normally liked their music loud and purposeful.

Johnson used his short time in Brazil to foster an alliance with that country's branch of the Surfrider Foundation. With his influence, several informational booths were set up at his concerts, which totaled more than 60,000 fans. He was also instrumental in organising a petition to stop the Brazilian government from dumping raw sewage into the ocean.

Johnson returned to Oahu in May to rest up for a tentative series of US dates set to begin in August and run through September. Johnson made no excuses for this rush of activity at a time when he was telling anyone who would listen that he was about to take some time off. To his way of thinking, it was not all talk and no action. He felt comfortable doing what he was doing and so he would proceed as planned. But he would continue to make the point that nothing was set in stone and that he could stop it all anytime he wanted.

During this period, Johnson once again began hearing the persistent rumour that Ben Harper and he were going to finally go into the studio and do an album together. Johnson acknowledged that it was his ambition to make such a record but that he did not see it happening anytime soon.

'We always talk about it,' he said in a *Ninemsn* feature. 'It's so easy to talk about doing it and both of us dream of doing it at some point. One of these days it will happen. Things will slow down for the both of us. I'd love to make a record with Ben.'

Harper, in an *UltimateGuitar.com* interview, was, likewise, amenable to doing an album with Johnson. 'If me and Jack Johnson were to make an album together, I'll be able to pull, he'll be able to pull and we'll also collaborate.'

With Johnson's fame at an all time high in 2006, he once again addressed the notion that the whole musical career had gotten too big too fast. But rather than speak in generalities, there was now a good-natured touch of weariness in his voice as he explained how tough it was getting to find privacy at the highest level of stardom.

'I'm starting to become a little bit (scared of it),' he said in the *Honolulu Weekly*. 'I started to feel the effect of it (celebrity) just in recent months of getting noticed on the beach and having people want to take a lot of pictures. To me, it's like when I go to the beach to surf, it's my time to go. I'm always real appreciative and I can't believe how nice people are about the whole thing. But it's a little weird to get stopped during the day.'

Fear of celebrity did not really seem to be the problem. The singer had cultivated an easygoing way of dealing with it and, when he wanted, avoiding its ramifications.

Fatigue, however, was beginning to weigh on Johnson's psyche. Johnson had always stated that when he's on the road or away from the surf for any length of time, he starts to feel out of sorts mentally. With the rush of activity in recent months and the near non-stop touring and recording of the past five years, those in Johnson's inner circle were beginning to see signs that Johnson was not his usual relaxed self.

When home, he would only pick up his guitar sporadically and then it was for recreational situations. No new songs were being written. As the head of his own label, there were certain business issues that had to be dealt with but, for the most part, he was delegating these assignments to his managers. When Johnson did focus on work, it would be to casually supervise the progress of other artists on the label. And even that was little more than shooting the breeze with friends or popping in and out of the recording studio to say hi.

Johnson was never what you would call moody but there were now moments where he was turning inward. Not that there was anything specific to point a finger at. The singer was good at concealing those deeper thoughts.

Johnson continued to keep the notion of a career at arms length. It often seemed that the more popular he had become, the more he was taking pains to distance himself from the success.

'I definitely thought it (music) was going to be a little break from the surf films,' he recalled in an *Associated Press* interview. 'And then it grew into something we started doing for the next couple of years. And now it's been on and off for the past five years.'

Johnson's weariness of the pop star grind could, seemingly, not have come at a worst possible time. With the growing popularity of the singer-songwriter, Johnson had come to be known, along with Ben Harper, Dave Matthews and a handful of others, as one of the foremost practitioners of the form. Barely into his thirties, he could afford to ride this wave of popularity for several more years and retire to Oahu a very rich and very young man. But to do that would have made his insistence on freedom at all costs a cop out of immense proportions. So while thoughts of compromise were often in his mind, the singer never gave into them.

By the end of April 2006, Johnson had made a decision. It was time to kick out. And this time he was serious.

12

Johnson Kicks Out

The announcement that Jack Johnson was taking a break came with a rather simple headline on the updates page of his official website:
Jack Johnson Plans To Take A Much Deserved Year Or Two Off From Touring And Recording.

It was all so low key in execution. No press conference. No final tour. It was as if Jack Johnson had awakened one day and simply decided that he did not want to do it anymore.

But by the time the first waves of disappointment were being heard from fans around the world, the cat was already well out of the bag. Weeks earlier, in an interview with the *Honolulu Advertiser*, Johnson told the reporter, during a bit of good natured banter about the pressures of the pop life, that he was serious about taking a big chunk of time off. Starting almost immediately.

'Yeah, this time it's gonna happen,' he said. 'This time it's for sure. We're going to take a whole year off and then maybe record another album. It'll probably be two years before I tour again. The Kokua Festival maybe the only show we do.'

Johnson went on to tell the *Advertiser* that his time off would consist solely of fun time in which he would occasionally go to other countries like Indonesia and Australia to surf but, otherwise, would pretty much stay home.

'I'm gonna be surfing as much as possible,' he said to no one's surprise. 'That's really it. I mean there's family time. But that just comes natural.

It's just the same as surfing.'

Of course Johnson had gone through the whole 'I don't want to do this anymore' song and dance so many times that few if any were taking this latest round of statements very seriously. Even those closest to Johnson smiled at the notion. Johnson wanting to pack it all in was just Jack being Jack.

Which meant that it came as little surprise when, not too long after those initial statements were made, Johnson qualified it all in a *Men's Journal* interview even as he was announcing that there will be no new album until at least 2008.

'I won't be able to record anything else for a little while. The songs will have to start coming again and if they do, they do. But it's not going to stress me out if they don't.'

Johnson, for the first time, hinted that a reason for his sudden hiatus was that he might have hit a creative wall. 'I go in phases,' he told *Men's Journal*. 'When I'm in tune, surfing all the time, then going out on tour sounds like fun. But by the end of the tour, I just want to start jockin' it and forget all about this music stuff.'

But even as he made those statements, there was much that was contradictory in his predictions of total creative inactivity.

'I'm always writing songs,' Johnson once said in a CD 101 FM interview. 'I write a bunch of songs. A lot of them I've never shown to anybody. Kind of just the way I think is always in rhymes. Anything that happens, I'll make a rhyme out of it. It's the way I remember things or answer the questions that are in my head.'

In that same interview, Johnson indicated that the creative well was far from running dry. 'I love writing songs. It's my favourite part of the whole gig. Sometimes I question performing but I never question writing songs. The entertainment aspect of what I do is kind of weird but writing the tunes is fun.'

All of which posited another hiatus scenario, in which new Johnson songs, most likely sung by Johnson himself, might appear on the occasional soundtrack or compilation album. After all, that kind of contribution would fall together fairly easily. The singer could easily knock out a song in a day and most producers would jump at the chance of having Johnson's fingerprints on their album.

'I've always tried to make it (music) secondary to life,' he told the

Associated Press. 'Don't get me wrong. I love music and it's something I hope I always do. But surfing is something that is kind of what brings my friends and I together.'

But there had to be more to Johnson's semi-retirement than mere hanging out. Reporters pushed for a deeper reason and found that a big reason for his temporarily calling it quits was that he was beginning to feel overwhelmed by the responsibilities of celebrity.

'This level of success has totally surprised me,' he admitted in an interview with *The Independent*. 'If I understood it (celebrity) too well, it would be dangerous because there'd be nothing left for me but to become a caricature. So it's definitely time to go home, put the guitar in the closet for a while and concentrate on other aspects of my life.'

Johnson was in no danger of understanding celebrity too well. Point of fact, while he understood the nuts and bolts of pop stardom, he was still largely a babe in the woods when it came to the impact his music and his presence was having on people. Much like his days as a photographer, Johnson was very much a point-and-shoot pop star. He just showed up and did his thing. He knew people liked his music but he was only now beginning to grasp the import of his music and his presence on the musical landscape as something beyond mere entertainment. It would not be too difficult to speculate that it was this sudden realisation that was making Jack Johnson want to run and hide.

When the majority of pop music acts take a break or, for that matter, call it quits, the response tends to be rather tepid in most cases. Pop fans, to a large extent, have a short memory and so, unless a band or musician has made a deep emotional connection, it's usually on to the next big thing.

With Jack Johnson, the jury was immediately out on his projected two-year absence from the public eye. His diehard fans acknowledged that he would be missed and not forgotten. But there was also a sentiment that Johnson had been a flash in the pan, albeit an entertaining and enlightened one, and that while he would be missed, there would not be an overwhelming demand for his return.

The more critical and cynical on the pop landscape were quick to acknowledge that Jack Johnson's entire career, despite his seeming naivety, had been a cold, calculating business move. It was a given that the singer had made more than enough money to live comfortably for the rest of his days and that his avowed hiatus was nothing more than a way to ease himself and his fan base into permanent retirement. As with everything else, Johnson had a good laugh at all the rumours and speculation and was moving quietly into his immediate future.

One possibility for Johnson's 'retirement' period was his often discussed desire to return to filmmaking. And on the surface, this was one theory that seemed to make sense. Johnson had long ago established a real love affair with the creative possibilities of film. His years in the spotlight had definitely given him a new perspective on the world, one that would most certainly add a new dimension to his approach to film and surf. The offers, from within the Malloy camp as well as elsewhere, had been coming in sporadically for the past few years and the notion of surfing the far reaches of the planet with some good buddies and chronicling their adventures for the world to see did retain its appeal.

But ultimately, when pressed, Johnson would respond with the importance of family as a primary reason for his stopping his career cold.

'The music has been great but now I have a kid so it's not so much about me,' he said in a *Strand/China Business Week* feature. 'I've got to reassess, step back and see what's best for him. If that means not touring ever again, then I won't.'

Truth be known, Johnson had other plans in mind for his semi-retirement besides surfing. He had long been concerned about the vast amount of beachfront property that was being bought up by Japanese developers. To combat the encroachment on his beloved coastline, and in particular one of his favorite spots, Sunset Beach, Johnson, along with surf buddy Kelly Slater and Oahu officials, had formed a corporation dedicated to buying back chunks of land from the Japanese. Johnson planned on spending much of his self-imposed career break working to get that land back. His immediate goal was to reclaim a 1,129 acre stretch of land known as Pupukea-Paumalu Bluff.

By the time Johnson had announced his vacation from the business, federal funding to the state had already contributed $7 million of the estimated $8 million that would be required to buy back that parcel of land and Johnson was determined to come up with the rest.

'These waves have pretty magical curves to them,' he said in a *Contactmusic.com* story, 'and development has proven to affect the water quality. Our goal is to protect the waves, the natural wonders. It's a big place in my heart. I'm just trying to hold onto it.'

And it was a goal that was very much on Johnson's mind during a press conference to publicise the conclusion of his Cans For Cash Challenge in which 25 schools competed in a recycling programme with Johnson making an appearance at the winning school.

'I think the main issue that everybody on this side of the island wants to see is just a little bit more energy put into the environment impact statement,' Johnson told the assembled media including the *Star Bulletin*. 'Anybody who has grown up out there or has spent a lot of time out there knows how much the North Shore has changed.'

Following the press conference, Johnson turned to a more joyous task, performing for the winning school, Punahou Elementary School. Johnson performed several songs for the thrilled youngsters, including his signature recycling song 'The Three R's'. He thanked the school for its recycling efforts. 'You might feel you're just little kids right now,' he said in a speech that was recorded for Punahou School Online, 'but what you're doing with recycling is actually teaching your parents, the older people, what they should be doing. Thank you for being the leaders of tomorrow and the leaders of today.'

Johnson also took the opportunity to encourage the students in their artistic endeavours. 'Whether it's music or painting or photography or surfing, whatever it is, just go ahead and follow your dreams.'

The gesture on Johnson's part to save his beloved island from corporate evil and his grassroots work on behalf of recycling was a telling point as the singer eased into the next phase of his life. There was a sense of relish and conviction that when, compared to his more sedate early approaches to recycling, was very aggressive in design and execution. Many considered the already outspoken Johnson's eco stance the next step to big time political activism in which he would become a leader in the fight to save the planet. Given his laidback, shy nature, one had to wonder if saving beachfront property in Oahu was the first shot fired in an increased presence as an activist? As with everything associated with the singer, it was just one of many speculative notions that Johnson was keeping in the air.

Despite his moratorium on performing, many wondered if Johnson would refrain from performing for good causes. The yearly Kokua shows were his creation and, in the intervening years, he had offered up his time to several benefit concerts. The consensus was that Johnson would continue to do those kinds of live performances but with Johnson nothing could be said with certainty.

Johnson's announcement of his 'break' from the world of music brought the expected uproar from the business side of his world. It was reported that promoters all across the country, who had counted on Johnson's presence to pack their venues, were now scrambling to fill a very big void in their 2006 concert schedule. The fears that pop stardom was a fleeting thing and that his absence would drive away his fans was voiced once again from the business side. And, like before, those fears were brushed aside by Johnson who sensed that the music industry were old hands at keeping a vacationing star in the public eye.

It was a safe bet that the old reliable stop gap greatest hits album would be hitting the stores round about Christmas. A collection of his music videos and the inevitable live album would also satiate his fans. And although Johnson would probably balk at the idea of releasing imperfect material, there were probably enough rough recordings, alternative takes and maybe a new song or two that never made the final cut to plug a hole in a release schedule if need be.

And Johnson was fine with those kinds of things being put out in his absence. While he would be the first to admit that not everything that he recorded was perfect, he would acknowledge that most of what had not been released was only a slight technical polish away from being eminently releasable.

One thing was certain, Johnson's inactivity was not going to leave his bandmates high and dry. Collectively and singularly, Podlewski, Topol and Gill were much in demand as session musicians and it was a safe bet that all would indulge themselves with solo albums and tours. Of course Gill would be very busy with the rising fortunes of Animal Liberation Orchestra whose stick had risen thanks, in large part, to exposure on Johnson tours.

There was also evidence to indicate that the Jack Johnson sound, considered by many to be a niche sound despite the millions of albums sold, was beginning to make its presence felt in more progressive circles. The biggest example of this was when Pink Floyd member David Gilmour sampled an Adam Topol drum sound (credited to Topol and Johnson) on the song 'In This Heaven' from his 2006 solo album *On An Island*.

Amid all the hoopla and speculation of Johnson going out on top, even for a while, the singer was having a good time teasing reporters about the authenticity of his retirement plans. On the one hand, he remained insistent that he would not be touring or recording for the distant future. But the nature of Jack Johnson has always been to go with the flow and, from time to time, well into 2006, he would drop little hints that in his world nothing was definite.

'I probably will get restless,' he told the *Honolulu Advertiser*. 'I always find that once I'm home for a few months, I actually get excited to go out and play again. And, by the end of the tour, I can't think of anything besides getting home and getting on a beach. So yeah, I probably will get a little restless and I'll probably go against everything I just said and actually be touring four months from now.'

While not actively involved in furthering his own career, the singer did find creative ways to spend his time as summer 2006 loomed. He was persuaded by director Jerry Aronson to sit still for an interview for the ambitious documentary entitled *The Life and Times Of Allen Ginsberg*. This was a labour of love for Johnson who emoted effusively on the influence the legendary Beat poet and philosopher had on his creative and professional life.

And Johnson's arm did not have to be twisted to go into the studio as a guest artist on G. Love's latest album *Lemonade*. It was a typical, hang-loose session with the likes of Ben Harper, David Hidalgo from Los Lobos, and Steven Molitz of Particle drifting in and out of the studio to add bits and pieces to what many consider Love's most accessible and commercially viable album in ages. The ease with which Johnson interacted with former label mate Donovan Frankenreiter, who also helped out on *Lemonade*, forever put an end to speculation that Frankenreiter's departure from Brushfire had caused a rift with Johnson.

Dutton, who initially had reservations about *Lemonade* turning into a 'heavy friends' session, had finally warmed to the idea. His interaction with Johnson on the cut 'Rainbow' was a particularly joyous collaboration and, although they had been constantly in touch over the years, for Dutton reuniting with Johnson in the studio was nostalgic. He would regale anybody who would listen with stories about how Johnson and he had gotten together.

'We're family,' he told *Billboard* in summing up his relationship with

Johnson.

Johnson would have preferred that his charitable good works not be made public. But occasionally he had no choice but to make an appearance and accept the accolades. One such case was in 2006 when Johnson and wife Kim were honoured as Environmentalists Of The Year by the Surf Industry Manufacturer's Association. At the ceremony, Johnson smiled uncomfortably for the cameras as SIMA Environmental Board Chairman Paul Naude proclaimed 'The Johnsons embody the word "Environmentalist." It is evident that they practice what they preach when it comes to protecting the environment.'

In recent years, Johnson had been very public in his charitable good works but by 2006, it was also becoming evident that every Jack Johnson contribution did not come with a built in photo op and press release. Such was the case when an announcement by the international charitable organization SurfAid on its website proclaimed that for the past year, Johnson, The Malloy Brothers and their film production company had been quietly donating proceeds from the sales of *The September Sessions* DVD, to date $118,000, to SurfAid and its work with the people of the Mentawi Islands in Indonesia to prevent diseases and to work with the island residents in recovering from natural disasters.

In another only slightly publicised contribution, Johnson contributed the song 'Bubble Toes' to a two-CD collection called *Sound Environment*. The charity collection, which also featured songs by the likes of Coldplay, Ben Harper, Missy Higgins and Bob Dylan, earmarked a generous percentage of sales to work for biodiversity in Australia.

And yet another by-product of his 2005 tour was gathering headlines in 2006 when it was announced that Johnson had donated generously to the National Energy Fund for the creation of energy producing windmills.

With very rare exception, Johnson stopped doing press in 2006. Although it was never clearly indicated as a reason for pulling back, it has been speculated that the notoriously shy singer was becoming increasingly uncomfortable with the press constantly probing into personal areas of his life. To be sure, Johnson's private life appeared beyond reproach, with the admission that he occasionally smoked a bit of the herb being the closest thing to sensationalism. True to his word, he had remained faithful to Kim even as the temptations of stardom grew. But he was often frustrated with the not-too-veiled tabloid approach many interviewers took and he was beginning to resent it.

'There are things that I've decided that it's okay for people to know,' he said in an interview with the *Honolulu Weekly*. 'It's a conscious effort to allow people to only know things I want them to know about me. Sometimes I find people have found out too much. But I don't have any secrets.'

The singer finally acknowledged one big reason for his saying goodbye for a while and it did not surprise that it was the simplest possible intrusion that had set Johnson off. Once he was in a position to do so, Johnson had always taken great pains to schedule his shows so that he might be able to get a bit of snowboarding and surfing in on his downtime. But with fame had come the increasing and not too subtle requests from promoters in which they asked the singer to sign a contract saying he would not risk injury before a show in their venue by taking to the slopes or the waves. For Johnson that was the last straw.

'I just look at them,' said Johnson in an interview with *The Independent*, 'and said "What do you think we came here for in the first place?"'

And so, in a very large sense, the Jack Johnson story had come full circle. In the beginning it was the record company executives who sought to bend and shape him. In the end it was the promoters who attempted the same thing. Johnson continued to be consistent. He continued to say no.

The Jack Johnson story is by no means complete. Baring any acts of God, he will return and continue to mesmerise audiences with his laid-back island style sometime in the future. But for now, the Jack Johnson story was ending pretty much the way it began.

Johnson was at home with his family and friends. He was on his long board riding the waves at Pipeline, the one place he was truly at peace. He was jumping on his beat-up bicycle and peddling along the shoreline to spend the day with his family and friends. In a year or two, his son may well be kneeling on his father's long board as he takes him out to the surf for the first time. However all of that can be nothing but speculation.

Because nothing is certain or permanent in the world of Jack Johnson. He's like the waves he rides. And that's where the magic is.

Discography

Albums

Brushfire Fairytales
Released: 2001
Inaudible Melodies, Middle Man, Posters, Sexy Plexi, Flake, Bubble Toes, Fortunate Fool, The News, Drink The Water, Mudfootball, F-Stop Blues, Losing Hope, It's All Understood.
Highest chart position:
Australia #13
UK #36

Thicker Than Water
Released: 2003
Moonshine, Rainbow, Even After All, Hobo Blues, Relate To Me, The Cove, Holes In Heaven, Dark Water and Stars, My Guru, Honor and Harmony, Liver Splash, Underwater Love, Thicker Than Water.
Did not chart.

On And On
Released: 2003
Times Like These, The Horizon Has Been Defeated, Traffic In The Sky, Taylor, Gone, Cupid, Wasting Time, Holes In Heaven, Dreams Be Dreams, Tomorrow Morning, Fall Line, Cookie Jar, Rodeo Clowns.
Highest Chart Position:
US #3
UK #30
Australia #2

In Between Dreams
Released: 2005
Better Together, Never Know, Banana Pancakes, Good People, No Other Way, Sitting Waiting Wishing, Staple It Together, Situations, Crying Shame, If I Could, Breakdown, Belle, Do You Remember, Constellations.
Highest Chart Position:
US #2
Canada #3
UK #1
Australia #1
New Zealand #1

Sing-A-Longs And Lullabies
For The Film Curious George
Released: 2006
**Upside Down, Broken, People
Watching, Wrong Turn, Talk Of
The Town, Jungle Gym, We're
Going To Be Friends, The Shar-
ing Song, 3 R's, Lullaby, My Own
Two Hands, Questions, Sup-
posed To Be**
Highest Chart Position:
US #1
Canada #1
UK #23
Australia #1

Singles (US and UK)

Flake
Released 2000
Highest Chart Position:
US Hot 100 #73
US Modern Rock # 22
UK Singles, did not chart

Bubble Toes
Released 2000
Highest Chart Position:
US Hot 100, did not chart
US Modern Rock # 39
UK Singles, did not chart

The Horizon Has Been Defeated
Released 2003
Highest Chart Position:
US Hot 100, did not chart

US Modern Rock #31
UK Singles, did not chart

Sitting Waiting Wishing
Released 2005
Highest Chart Position:
US Hot 100 #66
US Modern Rock #25
UK Singles, did not chart

Good People
Released 2005
Highest Chart Position:
US Hot 100, did not chart
US Modern Rock #29
UK Singles #50

Breakdown
Released 2005
Highest Chart Position:
US Hot 100, did not chart
US Modern Rock, did not chart
UK Singles #73

Sitting Waiting Wishing
UK Re-release 2005
Highest Chart Position:
UK Singles #65

Better Together
Released 2006
Highest Chart Position:
US Hot 100, did not chart
US Modern Rock, did not chart
UK Singles #24

Upside Down

Released 2006
Highest Chart Position:
US Hot 100 #38
US Modern Rock, did not chart
UK Singles # 36

Compilation Albums

Loose Change OST
Released: 2000
Songs: **Middleman, Mudfootball**

Out Cold OST
Released: 2001
Songs: **Posters**

The Perfect Day: 40 Years Of Surfer Magazine
Released: 2001
Songs: **Mudfootball**

Maybe This Christmas
Released: 2002
Songs: **Rudolph The Red-Nosed Reindeer**

MTV2 Handpicked Vol. 2
Released: 2002
Songs: **Inaudible Memories**

Bonnarro Music Festival 2002
Released: 2002
Songs: **Rodeo Clowns**

Aware 9: The Compilation
Released: 2002

Songs: **Posters**

Bonnarro Music Festival 2003
Released: 2003
Songs: **Wasting Time**

Austin City Limits Music Festival 2003
Released: 2004
Songs: **Taylor**

2003 Collection: Live From Austin, Texas
Released: 2004
Songs: **Taylor**

Mary Had A Little Amp
Released: 2004
Songs: **3 R's**

The September Sessions
Released: 2004
Songs: **Pirate Looks At 40, F-Stop Blues**

Handsome Boy Modeling School
Released: 2004
Songs: **Breakdown**

Look At The Love We Found: A Tribute To Sublime
Released: 2004
Songs: **Bad Fish / Boss DJ**

Some Live Songs
Released: 2004
Songs: Live all star jam with G.

Love, Donovan Frankenreiter and Kelly Slater

A Winter's Night
Released: 2005
Songs: **Rudolph The Red-Nosed Reindeer**

A Broke Down Melody OST
Released: 2006
Songs: **Let It Be Sung, Home, Breakdown**

Collaborations

Black Eyed Peas
Monkey Business
Released: 2005
Songs: **Gone Going**

Animal Liberation Orchestra
Alo
Released: 2005
Songs: **Fly Between Falls** (writer)

Filmography

Director
Thicker Than Water (2000)

Director
The September Sessions (1999)

Actor
Nice Guys Sleep Alone (1999)

Played: Woody

Actor
Endless Summer 2 (1994)
Played: Himself

Soundtrack Contributions

The Interpreter (2005)
Songs: **F Stop Blues**

Out Cold (2001)
Songs: **Posters**

Loose Change (2000)
Songs: **Middleman, Mudfootball**

Television Appearances

Grand Journal De Canal, Le (2006)

Top Of The Pops (2006)

Austin City Limits (2005)

Late Show With David Letterman (2005)

Saturday Night Live (2005)

Radio Music Awards (2003)

The Tonight Show With Jay Leno (2002)

Sources

As with any work of journalism, a number of sources contributed information, anecdotes and memories to the making of *Natural Born Man:
The Life Of Jack Johnson.*

I would like to personally thank Chris Mauro, Corky Carroll and Brian Shock for their insights and memories.

The following magazines and their professional journalists provided
invaluable information: *Surfer, Hooked On The Outdoors, Relix, Interview,
Rolling Stone, Outside, 20 Magazine, Launch, Time, Slap, Transworld
Skateboarding, The New Yorker, Q Magazine, Santa Barbara Magazine,
Guitar World Acoustic, Glide, Blender, Entertainment Weekly, UK Guitar-
ist, Happy Magazine, Paste, The Surfer's Path, Men's Journal* and *Chicago
Innerview.*

Likewise, the following newspapers proved excellent sources of information: *Honolulu Advertiser, Honolulu Weekly, Los Angeles Weekly, Los
Angeles City Beat, The Badger Herald, Daily Bruin, Chicago Tribune, Los
Angeles Times, The Sunday Mail, The Evening Standard, The Star-Bulle-
tin, Santa Barbara News-Press, Daily Trojan, The Independent, The Sunday Times, Maui Press, The Guardian Register, Oakland Tribune, Berkeley
Daily Planet, China Business Week* and *North County Times.*

These detail-oriented and information-rich websites were also valuable
sources: *Punahou School Online, Pop Rock and Jazz, Billboard.com, Swer.
net, Rolling Stone.com, Jack Johnson Music.com, Wikipedia, Beat A Go Go,
Barnes & Noble.com, Live Daily, MTV.com, South Florida.com, Synthesis.
net, Barfly.com, Contactmusic.com, Nashville City Paper.com, Coastalbc.
com, Surfing Vancouver Island.com, Daily Nexus, Outside.com, X Press Online, Independent.com UK, VH1.com, Sports Illustrated.com, Jack Johnson*

Online, Detours Online, Billboard.Biz, Brushfire Records.com, Ninemsn. com, This Is London.com, Internet Movie Database, CNN/SI.com, Obsurf. com, Ted Lennon.com, Radar Report, Yahoo Music.com, E Online, Global Village News, Sound Environment, Surf Industry Manufacturer's Association, Treehuggers.com, Jambands.com, Music In Schools Today Musicomh. com, Canoe, The Quicksilver Crossing and *ESPN.com.*

The following wire services, radio interviews and record company press materials also contributed invaluable information: *Mel In The Morning* Radio Show, 91 X San Diego Radio Interview, CD 101 FM, Associated Press and Universal Motown Record Group Press Release.

About The Author

Marc Shapiro is a full-time book author, freelance entertainment journalist, comic book writer and screenwriter. He has written more than 20 celebrity and entertainment books including the *New York Times* bestseller *J.K. Rowling: The Wizard Behind Harry Potter*. His previous music books have chronicled the lives of George Harrison, Carlos Santana, The Eagles, Lauryn Hill, Mariah Carey and Creed. Marc Shapiro lives with his wife Nancy in Monrovia, California, USA.

Forthcoming Titles From Helter Skelter Publishing

John Lydon's Metal Box: Stories From Public Image Ltd

by Phil Strongman
Paperback ISBN1-900924-66-8
256pp 234 X 156mm 16pp b/w photos
UK £14.99 US $19.95

Riots, sonic terrorism, all-out confrontation and the artist formerly known as Johnny Rotten in one of the few original Rock and Roll stories yet to be told. In between fronting rock's most iconoclastic group, the Sex Pistols, and re-emerging in the 21st century as a reality TV hero on *I'm A Celebrity*, Lydon led the post-punk pioneers Public Image Ltd, who tore up the rulebook and merged disco, funk and industrial punk to create coruscating soundscapes with catchy tunes - from 'Death Disco' and 'Flowers of Romance' to 'Rise' and 'This Is Not A Love Song' - and caused riots at their gigs. Featuring rare and exclusive Dennis Morris photos and extensive new interview material from the likes of Jah Wobble, this is an essential chapter in the growth of post-punk music; one that reveals Lydon as forever forward-thinking and always compelling.

Music In Dreamland: The Story Of Be Bop Deluxe And Bill Nelson

by Paul Sutton-Reeves
Paperback ISBN1-900924-04-8
384pp 234 X 156mm 16pp b/w photos
UK £16.99 US $25.00

Authorised biography of the flamboyant guitarist, singer and songwriter Bill Nelson, whose glam rock theatrics are revered and remembered by industry fans such as David Sylvian and the late John Peel. Be Bop Deluxe came to prominence during the 70s through a combination of rock theatrics and Nelson's fancy guitar work, moving from glam rock to new wave, via their art rock masterwork, *Sunburst Finish*. After Nelson split the band, he formed the acclaimed but short-lived Red Noise, with whom he recorded the new wave classic, *Sound On Sound* before embarking on a solo career. *Music In Dreamland* draws on hours of new interviews with Bill Nelson and other members of the band, as well as admirers such as Stone Roses' producer John Leckie, Steve Harley and Bowie's sometime guitarist Reeves Gabrel.

Wall Of Sound: A Phil Spector Reader

edited by Kingsley Abbott
Paperback ISBN1-905139-01-2
256pp 234 X 156mm 16pp b/w photos
UK £14.99 US $19.95
Currently accused of murder and awaiting a trial date, Phil Spector is the reclusive maverick producer who invented the 'Wall of Sound'. This collection gathers together the best articles, interviews and reviews about the enigmatic man and his revolutionary music by the editor of the acclaimed Beach Boys collection, *Back To The Beach*. At the forefront of the sixties pop explosion, Phil Spector was the man who raised the profile of the record producer to undreamed of heights. Using a combination of imagination, musicality and sheer chutzpah, his records became as important and influential as any from that exciting decade. His 'Wall Of Sound' was widely imitated, but never bettered, and the records he made with The Righteous Brothers, The Ronettes, The Crystals and Ike & Tina Turner are amongst the most played to this day.

Poison Heart: Surviving The Ramones

by Dee Dee Ramone
Paperback ISBN 1-905139-18-7
256pp 234 x 156mm 16pp b/w photos
UK £9.99
Revised and updated, *Poison Heart* is Dee Dee Ramone's perspective on 15 years touring with the band, following the ups and downs caused by the chemical and psychological imbalances it produced. It is a harrowing tale, both tragic and comic, littered with many of the colourful characters that made up the New York punk scene as well as cameos from John Cale and a gun-toting Phil Spector.

'*One of the great rock and roll books... This is the true, pathetic, awesome story of the Ramones.*' ***** **Q Magazine**

'*Dee Dee's story - knee deep in sex , drugs and rock 'n' roll is too incident packed to be anything less than gripping.*'**Mojo**

'Poison Heart *is like a Richard Price novel: full of delinquency, violence, addiction, brutality and ear-splitting rock 'n' roll.*'
Scott Rowley, The Band

Rock On Wood: Ronnie Wood
The Origin Of A Rock 'N' Roll Face
by Terry Rawlings
Paperback ISBN1-900924-80-3
288pp 234 X 156mm 16pp b/w photos
UK £9.99 US $18.95

Fully expanded and updated paperback edition of the definitive biography of one of rock's most distinctive sidemen, Rolling Stone, Ronnie Wood. Written with the cooperation of Ronnie Wood, his family and manager this book explores his life from childhood to his career with The Birds, The Jeff Beck Group, The Creation, The Faces and eventually The Rolling Stones. The 1999 hardcover edition omitted a great deal of information that didn't relate directly to the Stones. This 'director's cut' reinstates a wealth of material on Ronnie's musical exploits making it essential reading for anyone interested in 60s and 70s rock. Terry Rawlings is the acclaimed author of many books including *Mod: A Very British Phenomenon.*

David Bowie: The Shirts He Wears
by Jonathan Richards
Paperback ISBN 1-900924-25-0
288pp 234 X 156mm 16pp b/w photos
UK £14.99 US $19.95

A Bowie book with a difference, this is a psychological profile of Bowie as cultural icon that draws together his music, artworks and fashion to paint a fascinating portrait of one of rock's most important figures. The author looks at the many personae that Bowie has adopted and, drawing on a century of psychoanalytic learning, from Freud to latter-day cognitive thinkers, attempts to analyse Bowie the man and his turbulent personal evolution from a troubled childhood, through to his later drug abuse and flirtations with fascism, to happily married family man. The concept of the 'outsider' has been a constant in his work from 'Space Oddity' in 1969 to recent album *Reality* and his ever-changing appearance seems to confirm a restless curiosity, and perhaps search, for a real identity.

Let's Spend The Night Together
by Pamela Des Barres
Paperback ISBN 1-905139-17-9
256pp 234 x 156mm 16pp b/w photos
UK £9.99
Legendary groupie author of *I'm With The Band*, tells the full history of the groupie – girls who take their love of rock stars to the ultimate level. Beginning with the contention that Marie Magdelene was the first groupie, she charts the growth of literary 'muses' on to the rise of early rock pioneers like Cynthia Plastercaster, on to the phenomenon of 'models' marrying rock royalty, and on to the young groupies of today. Des Barres documents what it has meant to be a groupie and interviews many modern practitioners about what they do and why they do it. The first in-depth study of rock 'n' roll's ultimate fans.

Solid Air: The Life Of John Martyn
by Chris Nickson
Paperback ISBN 1-900924-862
256pp 234 X 156mm 8pp b/w photos
UK £14.99 US $19.99
First ever biography of versatile, genre-defying, pioneering guitarist, songwriter, hard-drinking hellraiser and ambient hero, whose best-known 70s album *Solid Air* is still hailed as a modern classic. Spanning an impressive five decades, Glasgow-bred, hard-man John Martyn's ongoing musical career has been as volatile as his hard-drinking life. A formidable guitarist, he innovated a unique musical style, incorporating echoes and effects to accompany slurred vocals that imitated the sound of a tenor sax and placed him somewhere between Eric Clapton and Tom Waits. Producing sometimes challenging and always emotional work since the 60s he has survived as a hugely acclaimed cult artist with crossover appeal. As well as collaborations with legendary ex-Pentangle double bassist Danny Thompson and Steve Winwood, Martyn's sound has taken in jazz, folk, blues, soul, dub and ambient. After a resurgent spell on Go Discs, he is now on the same independent label as Travis. Marred by health problems, Martyn recently overcame major surgery and continues to tour and record.

Linda Ronstadt: A Musical Life
by Peter Lewry
Paperback ISBN 1-900924-50-1
256pp 234 X 156mm 16pp b/w photos
UK £14.99 US $25.00

First book about one of country-rock's greatest stars. Ronstadt's early backing band became The Eagles and she enjoyed success with songs by Neil Young, Jackson Browne and Hank Williams. After a US number 1 single and Grammy-winning country rock albums in the 1970s, she has continued to challenge preconceptions with albums of Nelson Riddle-produced standards, a record of mariachi songs and a regular collaboration with Dolly Parton and Emmylou Harris under the name Trio.

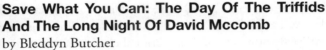

Save What You Can: The Day Of The Triffids And The Long Night Of David Mccomb
by Bleddyn Butcher
Hardback ISBN 1-900924-21-8
256pp 234 X 156mm 16pp b/w photos
UK £14.99 US $24.95

Finely crafted biography of cult Australian group and their ill-fated frontman who was simply the greatest lyricist of his generation. Charismatic frontman McComb's finely crafted tales of misfits, troubled outsiders and lost souls, merged Dylan with Carver and a Perth sensibility to brilliant effect, while his sprawling melodies set against 'Evil' Graham Lee's slide guitar created an achingly beautiful sound best exemplified by critics' favourites, *Born Sandy Devotional* and *Calenture*. In spite of rave critical plaudits, the Triffids' sales were mediocre and in 1990 the band split and returned to Australia. McComb put out one excellent solo album in 1994 before the sense of ominous foreboding that lurked throughout his music was proved prescient when he collapsed and was rushed to hospital to undergo a full heart transplant. Months later he was back in hospital with even more agonising intestinal surgery. McComb made a partial recovery, but the medication he was taking kept him in a permanent state of drowsiness. On Saturday, January 30th, 1999, he fell asleep at the wheel of his car. Though McComb survived the crash and discharged himself from hospital, he died suddenly three days later.

Rock Detector Encyclopedia Of Classic UK Rock

by Garry Sharpe-Young
Paperback ISBN 1-905139-06-3
512pp 234 X 156mm 8pp b/w photos
UK £16.99 US $25.00

In the 70s and 80s classic rock bands took the world by storm, re-inventing the international musical landscape across a whole breadth of styles and genres to incorporate blues, heavy metal, AOR and prog. Now, after the rise and fall of grunge and nu-metal, the classic rock brigade is back in force with bands such as The Darkness proving that catchy songs, long hair and guitar solos will always make for a winning combination. This book documents in the greatest of detail the histories and full global discographies of the groundbreaking acts Led Zeppelin, Deep Purple, Free, Yes, Queen, Emerson, Lake & Palmer, Bad Company, The Who and Black Sabbath et al. Every album is listed, with track list, catalogue number and international chart position. The second wave of platinum rock acts is also documented in exhaustive detail from Rainbow and Whitesnake, to Motorhead, and Saxon.

Rock Detector Encyclopedia Of Classic US Rock

by Garry Sharpe-Young
Paperback ISBN 1-905139-07-1
512pp 234 X 156mm 8pp b/w photos
UK £16.99 US $25.00

A companion volume to the classic UK rock encyclopedia that reiterates the fact that the classic rock brigade is back in force stateside too, with bands such as Velvet Revolver selling out shows regularly. Includes the histories and full global discographies of acts such as Van Halen, Boston, Kiss, Journey, Styx, Lynyrd Skynyrd, Vanilla Fudge et al. Every album is listed with track list, catalogue number and international chart position. The second wave of platinum rock acts is also documented from Guns N' Roses to Motley Crue and Bon Jovi as well as guitar heroes such as Steve Vai and Joe Satriani. Taking in the whole sphere of the classic rock genre, right up to Dream Theater and Velvet Revolver, this book is the only tome to give you all the information you could ever need.

The 100 Club: The First 60 Years
by Bob Brunning
Paperback ISBN1-900924-70-6
256pp 246 X 174mm 16pp b/w photos
UK £14.99 US $21.95
The 100 Club's history is the story of live music in England
- essential reading for anyone interested in jazz, blues,
punk, rock, reggae and world music. Since 1942 the 100 Club has been
a live music venue at the same site on London's Oxford Street. Following
its 1940s and 50s jazz and blues origins, the venue showcased legendary
60s American blues artists like Muddy Waters and BB King, key British
blues artists like Rod Stewart and John Mayall's Bluesbreakers, as well as
beat boom groups like The Who and The Kinks. The club was reborn
as the crucible of punk in September 1976 when it hosted the first ever
punk festival, featuring the Sex Pistols, The Clash, The Damned, Siouxsie
& The Banshees and The Buzzcocks. In the 1990s, the club became the
key indie music venue, featuring early shows from Suede, Oasis, Kula
Shaker and Travis. It has also remained at the forefront of reggae and
world music and hosted secret gigs and low-key warm-ups in recent years
by The Rolling Stones, Metallica and Paul Weller.

Flowers In The Dustbin: Sex Pistols
by Alan Parker
Paperback ISBN 1-905139-05-5
256pp 234 x 156mm 16pp b/w photos
UK £14.99 US $19.99
The year 2007 sees Parker issue his next volume on the Sex Pistols, *Flowers
In The Dustbin*. Presented as an alternative history to the group, *Flowers*
digs into the myth and exposes more truth than any other book available
on the group. In particular the book uncovers the real story behind the
relationship between Malcolm McLaren and skin flick filmmaker Russ
Meyer, a surface that's rarely been scratched in the past. Band members,
friends and employees have already been interviewed, in what promises
to be Parker's largest volume on the group to date. It will also feature
some unseen images; fasten your seat belts, the most dangerous ride in
rock 'n' roll just got more scary!

Action Time Vision: The Story Of Sniffin' Glue, Alternative Tv And Punk Rock

by Mark Perry
Paperback ISBN 1-900924-89-7
256pp 234 X 156mm 16pp b/w photos
UK £14.99 US $21.95

The legendary founder-editor of *Sniffin' Glue* - the definitive punk fanzine - gives his own account of the punk years. An eyewitness account of the key gigs; an insider's history of the bands and personalities; the full story of the hugely influential fanzine and the ups and downs of Perry's own recording career with his band Alternative TV. This is one of the few punk books that will have much to add to the canon as Perry tells the truth about the Pistols, The Clash, The Damned, the records and the rise and fall of punk rock.

Emerson Lake And Palmer: The Show That Never Ends

by George Forrester, Martin Hanson and Frank Askew
Paperback ISBN 1-900924-71-4
320pp 234 X156mm 100+ photos
UK £14.99 US $21.95

Revamped, revised, updated and expanded edition of the only biography of progressive rockers ELP, now featuring dozens of rare and previously unseen photos. Emerson, Lake and Palmer – their members drawn from King Crimson, The Nice and Atomic Rooster – epitomised the ambition of the progressive rock movement, mixing rock with jazz and classical music, introducing the synthesiser to the rock world and playing to huge stadium audiences across the globe. Drawing on years of research, the authors have produced a gripping and fascinating document of the prog-rock supergroup who remain one of the great rock bands of the seventies that also paints a vivid picture of an era of unparalleled showmanship, egomania and excess that will never come again.

'The musical analysis is surprisingly entertaining, even if like me you don' know your diminished fifths from your augmented wotsit.' **Classic Rock**
'The archetypal 70s prog-rock group, Emerson Lake and Palmer were as successful as any band of the era.' **Rough Guide to Rock**

Gram Parsons: God's Own Singer
by Jason Walker
Paperback ISBN 1-900924-75-7
256pp 198 X 129mm 8pp b/w photos
UK £9.99 US $17.99

B-format outing for the true, tragic story of Gram Parsons. He sang like an angel and dressed like a country star. Sadly he was neither – at least not in his own lifetime. Indeed Gram's short career was marked by a conspicuous lack of commercial success. Nonetheless, before his tragically early death, Gram played a key role in bringing together the worlds of rock and country music. He also made some stunning records. Freelance journalist and alt-country musician Jason Walker has spent seven years interviewing Gram's friends, colleagues and collaborators. The result is the most detailed portrait yet of the ill-fated rich kid who invented country-rock.

The Clash: The Return Of The Last Gang In Town (Revised)
by Marcus Gray
Paperback ISBN 1-905139-10-1
512pp 198 X 129mm 8pp b/w photos
UK £14.99

A revised edition of the exhaustively researched, definitive biography of the rock band whose instantly memorable hits 'London Calling,' 'Should I Stay or Should I Go' and 'Rock the Casbah' made them the greatest rock 'n' roll band of the post-60s era. The book vividly evokes the mid-70s environment out of which punk flourished, as the author traces their progress from pubs and punk clubs to US stadiums and the Top Ten. This edition is further updated to cover the band's recent induction into the Rock 'n' Roll Hall of Fame, band members' post-Clash careers and the tragic death of iconic frontman Joe Strummer.

'Revised edition of the superb band biography. Gray masterfully deconstructs The Clash's self-mythology. A fascinating, fiery read.' **** **Q**
'It's important that you read this book.' **Record Collector**
'A valuable document for anyone interested in the punk era.' **Billboard**

The Sharper Word: A Mod Reader (3rd Revised Ed)
edited by Paolo Hewitt
Paperback ISBN 1-900924-34-X
192pp 198 X 129mm
UK £9.99 US $19.95

Hewitt's hugely readable collection documents the clothes, the music, the clubs, the drugs and the faces behind one of the most misunderstood and enduring cultural movements and includes hard to find pieces by Tom Wolfe, bestselling novelist Tony Parsons, poet laureate Andrew Motion, disgraced Tory grandee Jonathan Aitken, Nik Cohn, Colin MacInnes, Mary Quant, and Irish Jack.

'An unparalleled view of the world-conquering British youth cult.'
The Guardian
'This is a great read.' **Mojo**

Into The Valley Of Offbeat Music: 100 Eccentric Music Makers And The Noise That Made Them
by Dave Henderson
Paperback ISBN1-902799-05-4
256pp 234X156mm b/w ill. throughout
UK £12.99 US $18.95

Essential reading for all connoisseurs of the musically strange. A journey into the underbelly of vinyl exotica that makes the guys from Hi-Fidelity seem like lightweights. Discover an odd netherworld of 100 innovative vinyl maestros who traverse the boundaries of style and common sense. They whistle, yodel and ramble. They make odd noises. They invent new chords. They are unique; they are in a record collection near you. They include a singing nun, Leonard Nimoy, Charles Manson, Harry Partch, Walter and Wendy Carlos and a whole load more. Dave Henderson is managing director of *Q, Mojo* and *Kerrang!* magazines.

No More Sad Refrains: The Life And Times Of Sandy Denny

by Clinton Heylin
Paperback ISBN 1-905139-11-X
352pp 198 X 129mm 16pp b/w photos
UK £9.99

Timely revised and expanded B-format outing for acclaimed biography of England's finest female singer-songwriter. Sandy Denny emerged from the 60s London folk scene to front Fairport Convention and also enjoyed critical acclaim for work with Fotheringay and her four solo albums as well as her vocal performance on Led Zeppelin's 'Battle of Evermore.' Sadly she struggled with drink and drugs and died tragically young aged 31 in circumstances surrounded by controversy.

'With intimate accounts from friends and colleagues, this is a bold but never sensationalised look at the finest British singer-songwriter of them all.' **Uncut**

'[This] is essentially yet another sex, drugs and rock 'n' roll tale, with stage fright and alcohol chasers.... Compelling.' **The Herald**

'No More Sad Refrains is also a welcome history of British folk-rock, or at least Denny's central role in the same. The sheer drama of her life never escapes author Heylin's grasp. Book of the month.' **Record Collector**

Passion Play: Ian Anderson And Jethro Tull

by Brian Rabey
Paperback ISBN 1-905139-03-9
288pp 234 X 156mm 16pp b/w photos
UK £14.99 US $21.95

New biography that documents the fascinating career of one of the most popular and enduring rock bands, Jethro Tull. Concentrating on the life and art of their founder and dominant creative force, fish farmer and country gent, Ian Anderson, this book draws on new interviews with the singer and his friends and collaborators to paint a fascinating portrait of one of rock's most distinctive frontmen and a legendary band. Tull combined rock with elements of folk music, not least frontman Anderson's virtuoso as a flautist, to become one of prog's biggest bands with million-selling albums such as *Aqualung* and *Thick As A Brick*.

Recent Highlights And Bestsellers

Steve Marriott: All Too Beautiful

Paperback ISBN1-900924-73-0
352pp 235X156mm 32pp photos
UK £14.99 US $19.95
Revised, expanded and updated edition of one of the most acclaimed music books of 2004: bestselling account of the Small Faces and Humble Pie mainman.

'The story of Steve Marriott is almost too awful to be true. Born in London's East End, he went from being fed jellied eels in his pram to teenage stardom as the lead singer of one of the most popular groups of the sixties, The Small Faces. After that there was success in America with his band Humble Pie and all the drugs and drink he could consume, three marriages and countless girlfriends and groupies and ever increasing penury. At the end he was to die at 44, if not penniless, poor, having generated millions for other people, burned to death in a fire at his home.' **Daily Mail**

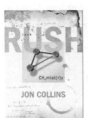

Rush: Chemistry

by Jon Collins
Hardback ISBN 1-900924-85-4
320pp 234 X 156mm 16pp b/w photos
UK £25.00 US $29.95
The first truly in-depth biography of one of the most enduring and successful cult bands in rock. Acclaimed Marillion biographer Collins draws on hundreds of hours of new interviews to tell the full story of the enduring Canadian trio who are one of the most successful cult groups in the world. From early days in Canada to platinum albums, stadium shows and the world's stage, taking in tragedy, triumphs and a wealth of great music, this is the meticulous and definitive study of one of rock's great enigmas. Against a background of media disinterest and a refusal to bow to mainstream industry marketing pressure, their success was by no means guaranteed. Only the determined efforts and downright stamina of the band members and those around them were sufficient to counter the wall of silence their originality encountered.

'Meticulous attention to detail... this authoritative book is engaging.'
Classic Rock

Belle And Sebastian: Just A Modern Rock Story

by Paul Whitelaw
Paperback ISBN 1-900924-98-6
288pp 234 X 156mm 16pp b/w photos
UK £12.99

First ever biography of the ultimate reclusive cult band – drawing on extensive interviews with band members. Formed in 1996, this enigmatic Glasgow band has risen to become one of Britain's most respected groups. For years, Belle and Sebastian were shrouded in mystery - the 8-piece ensemble led by singer-songwriter Stuart Murdoch refused interviews and the band scarcely toured. Their early singles though built them a strong and committed cult following. Their debut mail-order only album *Tigermilk* sold out within a month of its release and the follow-up, *If You're Feeling Sinister*, with its Nick Drake-influenced melodies and dark, quirky lyrics, found favour in alternative circles as far afield as San Francisco, Japan, South America and especially France.

'Frank account of their frequently eccentric career.' *****Q**
'Exhaustive research and plenty for fans to devour.' **NME**

Pink Floyd: A Saucerful Of Secrets (Post Live8 – Fully Updated)

by Nicholas Schaffner
Paperback ISBN 1-905139-09-8
352pp 198 X 129mm 8pp b/w photos
UK £10.99

From the psychedelic explorations of the Syd Barrett-era to 70s superstardom with *Dark Side Of The Moon*, and on to the triumph of *The Wall*, before internecine strife tore the group apart, Schaffner's definitive history also covers the improbable return of Pink Floyd without Roger Waters, and the hugely successful *Momentary Lapse Of Reason* album and tour. This revised edition contains a full update that covers in depth Pink Floyd's reunion performance at 2005's Live8 concert.

'Very nearly classic.' **Q*******
'Pink Floyd rarely let fans get past its walls; Schaffner has come from behind those walls with a worthwhile study.' **Rolling Stone**

Brian Jones: Who Killed Christopher Robin

by Terry Rawlings
Paperback ISBN 1-900924-81-1
288pp 234 X 156mm 16pp b/w photos
UK £12.99 US $19.95

The basis for Stephen Wooley's recent feature film *Stoned*, this first ever paperback of an out-of-print classic includes new photos of the movie set, new evidence and a deathbed confession. In 1969, The Rolling Stones' founder Brian Jones was found dead in the swimming pool of his home, Cotchford Farm, AA Milne's former residence. Through exhaustive research, Terry Rawlings has amassed evidence contradicting the official Accidental Death verdict and in this book he names Jones' murderer.

'The author has extensively researched Jones's life, from his teenage years fathering illegitimate children to forming the Stones and his eventual descent into drugged incapacity.' **Q**

Kicking Against The Pricks: An Armchair Guide To Nick Cave

by Amy Hanson
Paperback ISBN 1-900924-96-X
256pp 234 X 156mm 8pp b/w photos
UK £14.99 US $19.95

Complete career retrospective of one of the most important singer-songwriters of the last twenty-five years. *Kicking Against The Pricks* chronicles in depth the diverse personalities and the musical landscapes that Cave has inhabited, with a penetrating commentary on all his themes and influences. Cave's memorable collaborations and forays into other media are covered too: duets with Kylie Minogue, PJ Harvey and Shane MacGowan, the acclaimed novel *And The Ass Saw The Angel*, film appearances such as in Wim Wenders' *Wings of Desire*, and his stint as Meltdown 2000 curator. Ultimately, it reveals Cave as the compelling and always-relevant musical force he is.

'The slavishly in-depth dicography is perfect for dipping into, and also a fine reference work for completists.' **Classic Rock**

'This is a thoroughly competent Cave compendium'. **Uncut**

In Between Days: An Armchair Guide To The Cure
by Dave Thompson
Paperback ISBN 1-905139-00-4
256pp 234 X 156mm 16pp b/w photos
UK £14.99 US $19.95

The Cure's complete career, chronicled for the first time. *In Between Days* is the first book to make sense of a uniquely versatile band documenting their development from the new wave attack of 1979's 'Boys Don't Cry', the existential rock of *Seventeen Seconds* and the near-religious angst of *Faith* right up to the majesty of *Bloodflowers* and 2004's *The Cure*, consecutive 21st century masterpieces. Thompson also looks at Robert Smith's brilliant interweaving literary influences from Mervyn Peake and Coleridge to Albert Camus and Jean Cocteau.
'Meticulously researched and often unintentionally hilarious, thanks to Smith's curmudgeonly bitching, Not just for goths.' **Q**

'77 - The Year Of Punk And New Wave
by Henrik Bech Poulsen
Hardback ISBN 1-900924-92-7
512pp 246 X 180mm b/w ill. throughout
UK £25.00 US $30.00

Detailed history of all of the 200 UK (and Irish) punk or new wave artists who released a record or appeared on a compilation in 1977. As 1967 was to the Haight-Ashbury scene, so 1977 was to punk: a year in which classic singles and albums by all the key bands made it the only musical movement that counted, before its energy and potential was diluted and dampened by the forces of conservatism and commercialism. The story of what every punk and new wave band achieved in that heady year - from The Pistols, Clash and Damned to The Lurkers and The Rezillos, and everyone in between.
'For anyone wanting to relive the year that punk broke, this is a fantastic place to start.' **Rock Sound**
'This is a fantastic book... whether it's the Pistols or the Snivelling Shits, they all warrant their place because they made a record.' **Birmingham Post**
'An invaluable resource for any serious punk collector or scholar.'
***** **Record Collector**

Here Come The Nice: A Small Faces Songbook
edited by Paul Weller and John Hellier
Paperback ISBN1-905139-12-8
128pp 229 x 305mm b/w ill. throughout
UK £17.99 US $24.95
New collection of Small Faces songs selected and introduced by Paul Weller, with additional text by John Hellier and many rare photos. Features guitar-vocal arrangements of 'All or Nothing', 'Itchycoo Park', 'Here Come The Nice' and 12 other Small Faces classics.

'Weller and Hellier deliver something more than "just" a collection of sheet music and lyrics.' **Scootering Magazine**

'There's plenty on offer here, even for the non-musician.'
PlayMusic magazine

'Makes for both an enjoyable read and a practical guide to performing the band's music.' **Rockpile magazine**

From The Velvets To The Voidoids
by Clinton Heylin
Paperback ISBN 1-905139-04-7
288pp 234 X 156mm 16pp b/w photos
UK £14.99
Exhaustively-researched and packed with insights to give a detailed and all-encompassing perspective of American punk rock's 60s roots through to the arrival of new wave - this is the definitive story. Long overdue, fully revised and updated edition of the definitive account of the rise of US punk and the 'new wave' movement, led by acts such as Richard Hell, Television, The Ramones, Blondie and Talking Heads. This was originally published by Penguin in the early 90s. Clinton Heylin is the acclaimed author of a number of books including highly regarded biographies of Bob Dylan, Van Morrison and Orson Welles.

'No other book or account succeeded so well in accurately bringing the period to life.' **Richard Hell**

'Retains a real colour and sense of the era... makes for a fascinating read.'
PlayMusic magazine

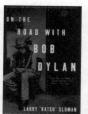

On The Road With Bob Dylan

by Larry Sloman

Paperback ISBN 1-900924-51-X

288pp 198 X129mm

UK £12.99

In 1975, as Bob Dylan emerged from 8 years of seclusion, he dreamed of putting together a travelling music show that would trek across the country like a psychedelic carnival. The dream became a reality, and *On The Road With Bob Dylan* is the ultimate behind-the-scenes look at what happened. When Dylan and the Rolling Thunder Revue took to the streets of America, Larry 'Ratso' Sloman was with them every step of the way.

'The War and Peace of Rock and Roll.' **Bob Dylan**

I'm With The Band: Confessions Of A Groupie

by Pamela Des Barres

Paperback ISBN 1-900924-61-7

320pp 198 X 129mm 16pp b/w photos

UK £9.99

Return to print for the ultimate story of sex, drugs and rock 'n' roll - the definitive groupie memoir from the ultimate groupie. From the day she peeked at Paul McCartney through the windows of a Bel Air mansion, Pamela was hooked. Graduating high school, she headed for the sunset strip and rock and roll. Over the next ten years, she dallied with Mick Jagger, turned down a date with Elvis Presley, had affairs with Keith Moon, Noel Redding and Jim Morrison, and travelled with Led Zeppelin as Jimmy Page's girlfriend - he had 'dark chilling powers' and kept whips in his suitcase. She hung out with Cynthia Plastercaster, formed the all-girl group the GTOs, and was best friends with Robert Plant, Gram Parsons, Ray Davies and Frank Zappa.

'Ah, those were the days, and this is still one of the most likeable and sparky first-hand accounts.' ******Q**

'Pamela's mixture of hippy enlightenment and teenage lust is terrific.' **The Guardian**

'I couldn't have done it better myself. I will always love you and, again, a thousand apologies for the premature ejaculation.' **Robert Plant**

'A kiss-and-tell that doesn't make you want to go and wash your hands.' **Music Week**

Everybody Dance: Chic And The Politics Of Disco

by Daryl Easlea
Paperback ISBN1-900924-56-0
288pp 234 X 156mm b/w ill. throughout
UK £14.00 US $19.95

The life and times of one of the key partnerships in musical history who were best known as the quintessential disco band Chic. Led by Black Panther activist Nile Rodgers and family man Bernard Edwards, Chic released and produced a string of era-defining records: 'Le Freak', 'Good Times', 'We Are Family', 'Lost In Music'. When disco collapsed, so did Chic's popularity. However, Rodgers and Edwards individually produced some of the great pop dance records of the 80s, working with Bowie, Robert Palmer, Madonna and ABC among many others until Edwards's tragic death in 1996. There are drugs, bankruptcy, up-tight artists, fights, and Muppets but, most importantly an in-depth appraisal of a group whose legacy remains hugely underrated.

'Daryl Easlea's triumphant Everybody Dance *is the scholarly reappraisal the "black Roxy Music" deserve.'* **Time Out**

Number 3 - Books of the Year, 2005. **NME**

Al Stewart: The True Life Adventures Of A Folk Rock Troubadour

by Neville Judd
Paperback ISBN 1-900924-76-5
384pp 234 X 156mm b/w ill. throughout
UK £14.99 US $19.95

Fully revised, expanded and updated paperback edition of the definitive biography of Al Stewart, the Scottish cult folk hero behind chart hit 'Year of The Cat' who enjoyed Top Ten success in the US. Leaning on extended interviews with Stewart - and many other 60s folk stars - this is a vivid insider's account of the pivotal coffee house scene which built the careers of Paul Simon - with whom Al shared a flat in 1965 - and many others, as well as a wry memoir of a 60s folk star's trials and tribulations through subsequent decades.

'The whole thing is a thoroughly absorbing read. Decidedly definitive.'
Record Collector

Recent Backlist

This Is A Modern Life compiled by Enamel Verguren
PB 1-900924-77-3 224pp b/w ill. throughout   £14.99 $19.95

Wheels Out Of Gear: 2-tone, The Specials And A World On Fire by Dave Thompson
PB 1-900924-84-6 256pp 16pp b/w photos   £12.99 $19.95

Electric Pioneer: An Armchair Guide To Gary Numan by Paul Goodwin
PB 1-900924-95-1 288pp 16pp b/w photos   £14.99 $19.95

Sex Pistols: Only Anarchists Are Pretty by Mick O'Shea
PB 1-900924-93-5 256pp   £12.99 $19.95

Psychedelic Furs: Beautiful Chaos by Dave Thompson
PB 1-900924-47-1 256pp b/w ill. throughout   £14.99 $19.95

Bob Dylan: Like The Night (Revisited) by CP Lee
PB 1-900924-33-1 224pp b/w ill. throughout   £9.99 $17.95

Isis: A Bob Dylan Anthology (Revised) edited by Derek Barker
PB 1-900924-82-X 352pp 16pp b/w photos   £9.99 $17.95

Smashing Pumpkins: Tales Of A Scorched Earth by Amy Hanson
PB 1-900924-68-4 256pp 8pp b/w photos   £12.99 $18.95

Got A Revolution: The Turbulent Flight Of Jefferson Airplane by Jeff Tamarkin
PB 1-900924-78-1 408pp 8pp b/w photos   £14.99

Love: Behind The Scenes On The Pegasus Carousel by Michael Stuart-Ware
PB 1-900924-59-5 256pp   £14.00 $19.95

The Fall: A User's Guide by Dave Thompson
PB 1-900924-57-9 256pp b/w ill. throughout   £12.99 $19.95

Be Glad: An Incredible String Band Compendium edited by Adrian Whittaker
PB 1-900924-64-1 288pp b/w ill. throughout   £14.99 $19.95

In Search Of The La's – A Secret Liverpool by Matthew Macefield
PB 1-900924-63-3 192pp 8pp b/w photos   £10.99 $17.95

Surf's Up: The Beach Boys On Record 1961-1981 by Brad Elliott
PB 1-900924-79-X 512pp 16pp b/w photos   £25.00

Get Back: The Beatles' Let It Be Disaster by Doug Suply and Ray Shweighardt
PB 1-900924-83-8 352pp   £9.99

Hit Men: Powerbrokers And Fast Money Inside The Music Business by Fredric Dannen
PB 1-900924-54-4 416pp   £14.99
'The best book ever written on the business side of the music industry... Unreservedly recommended.' **Music Week**

The Big Wheel by Bruce Thomas
PB 1-900924-53-6 192pp   £10.99 $17.95

Waiting For The Man: The Story Of Drugs And Popular Music by Harry Shapiro
PB 1-900924-58-7 304pp   £10.99 $18.95

Steve Diggle's Harmony In My Head by Terry Rawlings and Steve Diggle
PB 1-900924-37-4 304pp   £14.99 $19.95

Blues: The British Connection by Bob Brunning
PB 1-900924-41-2 288pp 40pp b/w photos   £14.99 $19.95

Al Stewart: Lights, Camera, Action - A Life In Pictures by Neville Judd
PB 1-900924-90-0 192pp b/w ill. throughout   £25.00 $35.00

Other Backlist

Ashley Hutchings: The Guv'nor And The Rise Of Folk Rock by Geoff Wall and Brian Hinton
1900924323 288pp   £14.99 $19.95

The Nice: Hang On To A Dream by Martyn Hanson
1900924439 256pp   £13.99 $19.95

Marc Bolan And T Rex: A Chronology by Cliff McLenahan
1900924420 256pp   £13.99 $19.95

Razor's Edge: Bob Dylan And The Never-ending Tour by Andrew Muir
1900924137 256pp   £12.99 $18.95

I've Been Everywhere: A Johnny Cash Chronicle by Peter Lewry
1900924226 256pp   £14.99 $18.95

Animal Tracks: The Story Of The Animals by Sean Egan
1900924188 256pp   £12.99 $18.95

Rock's Wild Things: The Troggs Files by Alan Clayson and J Ryan
1900924196 224pp   £12.99

Dylan's Daemon Lover by Clinton Heylin
1900924153 192pp   £12.00

XTC: Song Stories by XTC and Neville Farmer
190092403X 352pp   £12.99

The Nirvana Recording Sessions by Rob Jovanovic
0-946719-60-8 224pp   £20.00 $30.00

Prince: Dancemusicsexromance by Per Nilsen
0-946719-64-0 352pp   £9.99 $14.95

U2: The Complete Encyclopedia by Mark Chatterton
0-946719-63-2 320pp   £16.99 $24.95

To order any Helter Skelter publication or for further information on all Helter Skelter titles log on to:

www.helterskelterpublishing.com